Timeless Wisdom

A Collection of Karen Casey's Best Meditations

KAREN CASEY

▧ HAZELDEN®

Hazelden
Center City, Minnesota 55012-0176

1-800-328-0094
1-651-213-4590 (Fax)
www.hazelden.org

All text is reprinted with permission from *Each Day a New Beginning:
Daily Meditations for Women,* by Karen Casey (Center City, Minn.:
Hazelden, 1991); *Daily Meditations for Practicing the* Course, by Karen Casey
(Center City, Minn.: Hazelden, 1995); *Keepers of the Wisdom: Reflections
from Lives Well Lived,* by Karen Casey (Center City, Minn.: Hazelden,
1996); *A Life of My Own: Meditations on Hope and Acceptance,* by Karen
Casey (Center City, Minn.: Hazelden, 1993); *A Woman's Spirit: More
Meditations for Women from the Author of* Each Day a New Beginning, by
Karen Casey (Center City, Minn.: Hazelden, 1994); *Worthy of Love:
Meditations on Loving Ourselves and Others,* by Karen Casey (Center City,
Minn.: Hazelden, 1985).

Library of Congress Cataloging-in-Publication Data

Casey, Karen.
    Timeless wisdom : a collection of Karen Casey's best meditations /
    Karen Casey.
        p.   cm.
    Includes bibiographical references.
    ISBN 1-56838-736-9 (pbk.)
        1. Meditations. I. Title.
    BL624.2 .C38 2001
    158.1'28—dc21

                                                                2001024745

05 04 03 02 01   6 5 4 3 2 1

Cover design by Lightbourne
Interior design by Wendy Holdman
Typesetting by Stanton Publication Services, Inc

Timeless Wisdom

Dear Readers,

I was thrilled when my publisher asked me to select meditations from six of my books to create this anthology. My journey as a recovering woman has run parallel to my journey as a writer, and Hazelden has served as the midwife to this journey. I am ever grateful for this long-standing opportunity to serve other recovering people through my writing.

When I started writing my first book, *Each Day a New Beginning,* I didn't know where the process would take me. To my relief and delight, I discovered that writing provided me with a release for my worries and a sure way to connect to a Higher Power.

Since then I have written fourteen more books, all of which called me "to the table" to listen to my Higher Power and challenged me to reach out to others. Through the Twelve Step fellowship, I have learned that the messenger within wants to speak to each of us. Becoming a writer has been as simple, and as necessary, as that for me. I believe each of us is blessed with an inner messenger. Whether or not we choose to listen makes the difference between having a life of serenity or a life of turmoil.

As you might imagine, my life has not remained in a state of total serenity. Even though I have celebrated twenty-five years of continuous recovery, I have weathered many storms. In many cases, these storms have given rise to new books. Over and over I have discovered that the message of my Higher Power calms me as long as I am willing to listen and share the insights.

I hope, dear friends, that this anthology of meditations offers you peace and hope as you walk through the next year of your life. It is my sincere wish that you will choose to carry some of your own peace and hope to others in your daily journey. I also hope you will turn within for direct communication with the God of your understanding. The journey is softened for all of us each time even one of us chooses to listen and be moved by what we hear. May Peace be with you.

—KAREN CASEY

Timeless Wisdom

January

January 1

What do we live for, if it is not to make life less difficult for each other.

—GEORGE ELIOT

Always seeing our struggles as the fault of others is a good indication that we need an attitude adjustment. There is no better place to get one than in this program of recovery. The women around us and the Steps that guide us can help us discover the joy of cultivating a new attitude.

Trying to determine the grand purpose of our lives can be overwhelming and anxiety-provoking. As alcoholics, we gravitate toward complicating the simple. That's why one of our slogans is "Keep it simple." We can apply this to all our relationships. Asking ourselves what we can do to help someone else, at every opportunity, defines our purpose in life quite clearly. Moment by moment, we'll never doubt what to do next.

My purpose is to help someone else today. If I think someone is causing me a problem, perhaps I should address my attitude.

—from *A Woman's Spirit*

January 2

*... that is what learning is. You suddenly under-
stand something you've understood all your life, but
in a new way.*

—DORIS LESSING

As we are changed by our experiences, that which we know
also changes. Our experiences foster growth and enlightenment, and all awarenesses give way to new understandings. We are forever students of life blessed with particular
issues designed only for us. There is joy in knowing that
learning has no end and that each day offers us a chance to
move closer to becoming the persons we are meant to be.

To understand something more deeply requires that
we be open to the ideas of others, willing to part with
our present opinions. The program offers us many opportunities to trade in the understandings we've outgrown.
Throughout our recovery we have discovered new inter-
pretations of old ideas. And we will continue to expand
our understanding.

Every situation, every person, every feeling, every idea
has a slightly different hue each time we encounter it. The
wonder of this is that life is forever enriched, forever fresh.

*Each moment offers me a chance to know better who I am and to
understand more fully the real contribution that is mine to make
in this life. I will let the anticipation of my changing ideas excite me.*

—from *Each Day a New Beginning*

January 3

Live and let live is good advice.

The more comfortable we are with the knowledge that each of us has a unique journey to make, a specific purpose to fulfill, the easier it is to let other people live their own lives. When family members are in trouble with alcohol or other drugs, it's terribly difficult to let them have their own journey. Because we love them, we feel compelled to help them get clean and sober. In reality, all we can do is pray for their safety and well-being. Their recovery is up to them and their Higher Power.

For some of us it's a leap of faith to believe there really is a Divine plan of which we are all a part. And perhaps it's not even necessary to believe. But we'll find the hours of every day gentler if we accept that a Higher Power is watching over all of us.

Being able to let others live and learn their own lessons is one of our lessons. The more we master it, the more peaceful we'll be.

I have enough to do just living my life today. I can let others do what they must.

—from *A Life of My Own*

January 4

Life is not what you did. It's what you are doing.
—JIM BURNS

Today awaits our attention and involvement. We can sit and merely ponder the possibilities for action, thinking away the entire day. We could get involved in a volunteer effort; we always said we would when time allowed. We could reorganize the basement, the kitchen, the garage. Our lives allow for spontaneous pursuits now. Or we can keep our focus small, taking each hour as it comes and reaching out to at least one other person in every sixty-minute span of time, doing nothing major, simply expressing our aliveness.

Maybe it's a phone call that keeps us connected to the human community. Or perhaps it's writing a long overdue letter. Offering a hello and a smile to a neighbor or a fellow shopper quite specifically strengthens our connection to the human community. It's not what we do that's so important. Rather, it's making at least one human contact with another living soul that will benefit all of our lives today.

Being too busy to let others know how much they matter to me isn't a problem any longer. Every day offers me opportunities to connect with others.

—from *Keepers of the Wisdom*

January 5

We are exactly where we need to be right now.

It's good to be reminded that we are where we need to be, particularly if we're prone to think we are missing out on some opportunity or fearful that we aren't making significant progress in our careers or other areas. When we doubt that we're doing enough in any regard, this principle helps us quiet down and ready ourselves to peacefully do the right thing. It will always surface.

It's comforting to realize there are no accidents, no coincidences happening in our lives. What we need to experience, to learn, to teach, in order to complete our journey home, will spring forth when the timing is perfect. We'll never have to search in vain for our next assignment. It will capture our attention.

There is never a need for lamentations. If we haven't fulfilled some task to our satisfaction, we can redo it. Now. If we haven't treated a companion or co-worker respectfully, we can make amends. Now. There isn't anything complicated about how to move through this day or these activities. We simply need to walk with the Holy Spirit and we'll get to our destination on time.

There are no mistakes in what comes my way today. How I respond depends on who I ask to help me see the circumstances.

—from *Daily Meditations for Practicing the* Course

January 6

Each day is a "workshop." Let's remember to keep our minds and hearts open so we won't miss our opportunities.

—DUDLEY MARTINEAU

Looking at every day as a workshop for more productive or rewarding living eases the dread of new or unfamiliar circumstances. Developing the belief that we will be given exactly what we need to learn will change how we meet every twenty-four hours.

Before recovery we expected life to be hard. Our jobs often felt like drudgery. Our families seldom gave us the affirmation we longed for. Friends were unavailable. What we felt we deserved and sought, we often didn't find. That was then. This is now.

It's a simple change in perspective to come to believe that we are given what we need from our jobs, our families, our friends, every day. Accepting this belief will influence the outcome of every experience. Our lives will never seem the same.

I paid my dues for today's workshop by becoming abstinent. What I learn is up to me.

—from *A Woman's Spirit*

January 7

Of course, fortune has its part in human affairs, but conduct is really much more important.

—JEANNE DETOURBEY

It's not infrequent that we are faced with a dilemma; what is the best action to take in a certain situation? We can be guided, rightly, in every situation if we but turn inward and let our conscience direct our behavior. We have often heard it said at meetings that when we long for a message from God we will hear it, either through our conscience or in the words of our friends. Thus we can never really be in doubt; our conduct can always be above reproach if we but listen.

Right behavior leads to fortunate opportunities for those who look for them. Behavior that we're proud of seems to attract blessings in our lives. One's good fortune is really God-given and in proportion to one's willingness to act well toward others in all situations.

Simply, what goes around, comes around. Our behavior comes back to us, manyfold. In our encounters with others today, we'll have numerous occasions to decide about the best behavior for the particular circumstance. We must not forget that our behavior elicits the responses we receive.

I will invite blessings today. I will also shower blessings on my friends.

—from *Each Day a New Beginning*

January 8

No decision has to bind us forever.

Most of us are no longer sure what we want to be doing a year or even a month from now. When we are called upon to make decisions that commit us to a certain path in the future, we shudder. Will we be allowed to change our minds?

What a change this is from earlier years. Many of us led very controlled lives. We felt safest when we knew exactly what we were going to do. We liked it best when we were able to control others' lives too, even though we failed at that much of the time.

Although we may have responsibilities at work and at home, we are so much freer now. And we can decide, moment by moment, what we *need* to do for ourselves. At first it feels irresponsible, not being responsible for everyone, changing our minds when we need to. However, we will grow into this new way of living. And we'll love it!

My decisions today will be for this day only. I can change my mind tomorrow.

—from *A Life of My Own*

January 9

Example is the lesson that all men can read.
—GILBERT WEST

Patterning our lives after others is familiar. Maybe as kids we emulated "toughies" or the teacher's pet. As we grew, the criteria changed, but we sought role models, nonetheless. The career we chose and the family relationships we developed may have been inspired by the example of another. Today may be no different. Seeing our friends and acquaintances pursue paths unlike our own gives us ideas to explore. How lucky we are that teaching is never done and learning is merely a decision.

The only thing that has actually changed is our age. The opportunities for growth continue to flow. Our purpose for being here remains the same. Our responsibility to ourselves never abates. It's comforting to count on these things. It makes our choices simpler.

There's always the right step to take, the right response to make, the right attitude to foster. But if ever we're in doubt, the impulse to forgive and to love will never be wrong.

My action today may be an important example for a friend. I pray to choose my steps and words wisely.

—from *Keepers of the Wisdom*

January 10

Miracles result from a shift in our perceptions.

Every expression is either one of love or a cry for healing and help. Remembering this simplifies how we experience life. The most difficult of circumstances reveals a far simpler lesson than we might imagine when it is perceived through loving eyes and a forgiving heart.

But what of the abuse, physical or emotional, we may have suffered at the hands of parents or spouses? Can those experiences be forgotten, forgiven, or simply explained away? *A Course in Miracles*® teaches us that every unloving action is always a cry for healing and help. Regardless of its intensity, an act that hurts us is a cry for help that has grown out of fear.

Embracing this truth doesn't come easily at first. Maybe we can accept it in a few situations. A friend's putdown or the bus driver's rude remark can be overlooked. But the more serious circumstances require our willingness to suspend all judgment and offer only forgiveness instead. With time and practice this will become easier.

I will quietly think through an action before I take it today. I will ask myself, Is this action loving?

—from *Daily Meditations for Practicing the* Course

January 11

*The love, the acceptance of other persons makes me
into the unique person I am meant to be.*

—PETER G. VAN BREEMEN, S.J.

Our destinies are fulfilled through our loving involvement
with the men, women, and children sharing our experience. It is not by accident but by design that we've been
drawn together to share goals, the workplace, or a home.
We contribute to each other's search for understanding,
and the spiritual quest that's at our center finds its resting
place in one another's hearts.

The letter, the smile, or phone call we offer a fellow
traveler today will bless our own faltering steps throughout the long hours ahead. Each time we focus our attention on the struggle or joy of someone else, our personal
well-being is enhanced. If we give away our love, we'll doubt
less that we, too, are loved.

—from *Worthy of Love*

January 12

Choices are not irrevocable. . . . They can be remade.

—JULIE RIEBE

Knowing that we can make choices about every circumstance in our lives fills us with awe at the breadth of our personal power. For decades, perhaps, we felt we had none. Life was bleak and we were at its mercy. How thrilled we are to understand, finally, where our power begins.

We are learning so much from this program. At times we wonder how we survived for so long on so little understanding. Our condition felt hopeless, and because we took no responsibility for changing our circumstances, nothing changed.

That's true no more. Every day we intentionally make choices about what's happening in our lives. Some choices, like changing a job or confronting a friend, are big. Others, like deciding whether to exercise today or tomorrow, are small. Large or small, our choices allow us to decide who we are, and none of our choices are without significance. That's exciting!

I will choose carefully today. If a change of mind is in my best interest, then I can change my mind.

—from A Woman's Spirit

January 13

*If I can stop one heart from breaking, I shall not live
in vain; If I can ease one life the aching, Or cool one
pain, Or help one fainting robin Into his nest again,
I shall not live in vain.*

—EMILY DICKINSON

The gift of attention to each other is "passing on" the love
of God. In order to feel love, we have to give it away. We will
know love when we give love.

Our attachment to the world, the sense of belonging
most of us longed for the many years prior to recovery,
awaits us, is showered upon us even as we reach out to
someone else. We are no longer alone, scared, alienated
when we let others know they are not alone. We can heal
one another. The program opens the way for our healing.

Each day, each one of us can ease the pain of a friend, a
co-worker, a child. The beauty of the program, the beauty
of God's plan for us all, is that our own pain is relieved in
the process of easing the pain of another. Love is the balm.
Loving others makes our lives purposeful.

No day is lived in vain, if I but cherish someone else's presence.

—from *Each Day a New Beginning*

January 14

Letting go is a decision.

The obsession to pressure other people to see things our way keeps us agitated. In contrast, the wisdom to understand that every person's view has validity, at least for that person, is a gift we receive from working the Twelve Steps. Our daily assignment, then, is to be patient and listen so that we may learn this lesson from women and men who have walked this path already, women and men who have come to understand that letting go of others and their addictions promises relief from the obsession that troubles each of us.

Look around. No one came to this particular juncture in the road because it was a hoped-for destination. Each of us ended up here because of our pain. All of us tried to force solutions that didn't fit. And we drove ourselves crazy trying to control the behavior of others, certain that "doing it our way" was not only reasonable, but right. Our past sometimes may appear to be a series of failures. But our present experience can be peaceful, hopeful, and successful. It's our decision to let go. A small decision that we can make many times today. Every day.

Let go *are tiny words with huge rewards. If I want to, I can give up my attempts to control someone today. Peace will be my reward.*

—from *A Life of My Own*

January 15

As you grow older, try to grow kinder and more broad-minded and more generous.
—ALPHA ENGLISH

As we age, our athletic ability declines. Our memory fails us more often. We tire more quickly, too. And developing the enthusiasm to explore uncharted territories requires more effort than when we were young. However, in spite of these admitted shortcomings of old age, we are never too tired or too forgetful or too bored to be kind to our friends and fellow travelers. Indeed, this is one area that we can show marked improvement in as we advance in years.

Knowing that we can get better at some things is exciting. The good news is that we can practice these attributes as often as we want. Every encounter with another person gives us the chance we need to be kind. Being more open-minded to the opinions of others is also a decision. And maybe we can't be more generous financially, but we can always be more generous in spirit. That's of even greater value to the well-being of the human family. Growing old *is* growing better. We can see that now.

I will have many opportunities to hone my skills today. Each person I encounter will be the better for it.

—from *Keepers of the Wisdom*

January 16

God's voice is present even when we're not listening.

It's beneficial to know that God never leaves our side. Obviously we don't always listen to His guidance. And even when we do, we neglect to follow it sometimes. If we followed it, we'd experience every situation in our lives far more peacefully. However, recognizing God's presence even once is a beginning. Any change we make in this regard strengthens our willingness to listen to God more quickly the next time we're feeling indecisive.

What keeps us from listening to the words of God? For most of us, the interloper is the incessantly nagging ego. It drowns out the Holy Spirit. Unfortunately, we're never benefited by the ego's suggestions, but it keeps us too busy to evaluate our actions. We mistake busyness for worthiness, perhaps. Let's remember we are always worthy in God's eyes. It's the ego that labels us unworthy.

We'd be so much happier, so much more peaceful, if we gave our total attention to the Holy Spirit. Can that be so hard?

Today's activities will trip me many times unless I keep my mind on God. Any discomfort I have is my clue my mind has wandered.

—from *Daily Meditations for Practicing the* Course

January 17

*We will never hear anyone else's thoughts if we are
only listening to our own.*

—CATHY STONE

It's not a defect to think. On the contrary, we need to ex-
amine all the issues in our lives, evaluating very carefully
what action to take in each instance. Many of us are still
clearing up the mayhem that occurred because we didn't
give enough thought to situations in the past. But there is
nothing gained by constant self-analysis, particularly during those moments when God has sent a friend to share
with us her story or perspective.

It's never an accident when another person discusses
with us an experience she has had. God intends for us to
learn from one another. We are students and teachers,
interchangeably. When a teacher comes our way, let's put
our minds to rest. Her words may supply the answer we
seek.

*I will be drawn to the people who have something to teach me
today. I will listen first and think later.*

—from *A Woman's Spirit*

January 18

At fifteen life had taught me undeniably that surrender, in its place, was as honorable as resistance, especially if one had no choice.

—MAYA ANGELOU

We had to surrender to a power greater than ourselves to get to where we are today. And each day, we have to turn to that power for strength and guidance. For us, resistance means struggle—struggle with others as well as an internal struggle.

Serenity isn't compatible with struggle. We cannot control forces outside of ourselves. We cannot control the actions of our family or our co-workers. We can control our responses to them. And when we choose to surrender our attempts to control, we will find peace and serenity.

That which we abhor, that which we fear, that which we wish to conquer seems suddenly to be gone when we decide to resist no more—to tackle it no more.

The realities of life come to us in mysterious ways. We fight so hard, only to learn that what we need will never be ours until the struggle is forsaken. Surrender brings enlightenment.

Life's lessons are simple once I give up the struggle.

—from *Each Day a New Beginning*

January 19

Our teachers surround us.

When we were young, our parents and siblings served as our teachers, but they weren't always good ones. We may have learned habits that haunt us still. Shame and guilt may still trouble us because of the messages our parents and siblings gave us. We can't undo the past teachings, but we can come to believe those teachers did their best. They passed on to us what they had been taught. Fortunately, the Twelve Step program can help us discard behaviors that serve us no more and cultivate ones that do.

We're students of life and we'll encounter many teachers. From some, we will learn patience; from others, tolerance and acceptance. A few will make us laugh. All will change us in some way. We may be apt to pass judgment on the interactions we have with others, but those with more wisdom than ourselves remind us that we can learn. In fact, we are privileged to learn something of value in absolutely every interaction. Our teachers are all around us.

I will accept that every person is my teacher today. I may be in for many surprising lessons!

—from *A Life of My Own*

January 20

❧

Sometimes two minuses make a plus.
—EDITH SHANNON

What appears to be a problem sometimes turns out to be a most beneficial circumstance. We live only in the present, and it generally takes the perspective of hindsight to get the full meaning of an event. Over the years, we have learned that some of our best lessons actually caused us pain while we were in their clutches. What a relief to be able to see, now, that they had their silver lining. This principle still holds true.

We have had a lot of years to learn to take our experiences in stride, giving them no more weight than they deserve. But it's easy to forget that it's the accumulation of them all that defines who we are. The lost jobs, the friends who left, the hurdles in a marriage all played their part in the people we've become today. We are who we need to be right now.

I can't let a setback set me back today. Whether I'm sixty or seventy or eighty, I am evolving right on schedule.

—from *Keepers of the Wisdom*

January 21

Seek peacefulness.

Few of us would admit to wanting anything but peace. Why then does it evade us so often? We hear repeatedly that we receive that which we seek. Do we not seek peace? Obviously we do not. What we think we want and what we obsess about are frequently far different. The latter is what we get.

The formula for discovering peace is simple. Try the following: stop thinking. Get quiet. Turn your attention to the Spirit within and ask for clarity, for a different perspective, for a forgiving heart. *Peace will come.*

If it's so easy, why aren't we surrounded by more peaceful companions? Because the noisy ego is so seductive. It clamors for our attention just as it clamors for control of our lives and the lives of others. The ego convinces us we'll be more secure if it's in charge. Painfully learning, again and again, that that's not the case eventually leaves an indelible mark. Peace will seek us then.

My journey will enlighten me today if I'm attentive.

—from *Daily Meditations for Practicing the* Course

January 22

In real love you want the other person's good. In
romantic love, you want the other person.
— MARGARET ANDERSON

The expression of real love is so easy between grandparents
and children—and between good friends it passes effort-
lessly. But why is it so hard to share real love with a spouse
or lover? Why, instead, do we want to possess them? And
from them we dream of selfless devotion. Yet neither possession nor devotion guarantees the security we long for.

Real love is not selfish; it frees both the giver and the
receiver. Knowing we're loved sustains our hearts and diminishes our difficulties. It doesn't bind us, yet paradoxically it bonds our hearts. This encouragement to grow, to
change, to dare to depart if it's for our own good, are expressions of real love. Real love is never ownership, only
stewardship of this moment's experiences.

Let's be gentle with one another, and love fully with
trust, as a child loves a grandmother.

—from *Worthy of Love*

January 23

We honor the spirit in other people when we listen to them.

God's messages surround us. The twenty-four hours before us are special, never to be repeated. The people we share the day with carry our lessons within their words and actions. Let's be vigilant in our attempts to listen.

We have so much to learn, and that's why we're here. Our lives have purpose, even though we might fail to grasp it. Remembering that God is trying to reach us in even the most mundane of circumstances keeps us attentive to everyone in our lives. Our attention to others triggers their lessons too.

The cycle is never-ending. We are not here by accident, we are here by design. The role addiction plays in our lives is part of the design. We can learn our lessons and fulfill our purpose only by acknowledging the spirit, the presence of God, within each person God has ushered to us.

I will pay special attention to the people in my life today. It's a wonderful feeling knowing they are part of God's plan for me.

—from *A Life of My Own*

January 24

To keep a lamp burning we have to keep putting oil in it.

—MOTHER TERESA

Our spiritual nature must be nurtured. Prayer and meditation lovingly kindle the flame that guides us from within. Because we're human, we often let the flame flicker and perhaps go out. And then we sense the dreaded aloneness. Fortunately, some time away, perhaps even a few moments in quiet communion with God, rekindles the flame.

For most of us, the flame burned low, or not at all, for many years. The flickering we may feel today, or tomorrow, or felt yesterday, will not last, so we may put away our fears. We can listen to the voice of our higher power in others. We can listen, too, as we carry the message. Prayer surrounds us every moment. We can fuel our inner flame with the messages received from others. We can let our spirit spring forth, let it warm our hearts and the hearts of others.

We each have a friend whose flame may be flickering today. I will help her and thus myself. A steady flame can rekindle one that's flickering.

—from Each Day a New Beginning

January 25

❧

The scarcity principle governs too many lives.

We lack nothing. We certainly don't think that and we don't live as though that's true, but, in fact, we are perfect, whole in every way, loved totally by our Creator, equal to everyone we see. Unfortunately, we don't see ourselves through God's eyes so we assume we are flawed, inadequate, not worthy of the love we crave from others.

How dark we have made this world we see. At times, we wonder if it will ever change, if we will ever change. At those times, let's look closer at the friends we admire. Perhaps they see a sunnier side of life. It's important that we understand we have the same capabilities as everyone else. We are everyone else! To see a lighter side of something, we need only ask for another view. By carrying our dark perception to the light, to the Holy Spirit, we'll garner another vision. The rapidity with which we do this defines how long our world looks dark.

I lack nothing today. The Holy Spirit guarantees me guidance and safety and love.

—from *Daily Meditations for Practicing the* Course

January 26

I have come to realize that all of my fears are false gods before me.

—MARY CASEY

Some days are free of fear: they flow smoothly with not a single "tremor." What's different on those days? Without realizing it, we probably left God's work to God. Fears generally surface when we get too personally invested in the outcomes of situations and in the actions of people we care about. We get confused and think our well-being is dependent on them and what they do rather than on God.

Fear about anything is the same as denying God's presence in our lives. It's not easy to shake the fear from our minds once we have given in to it, but we can if we follow the suggestions of this program. Most of us have come to believe in a Higher Power. Remembering to rely on that Power, letting it take charge of our lives and will, is our most positive option.

Any fear I have today is of my choosing. Dwelling on God rather than on the fear will change every experience I have today.

—from A Woman's Spirit

January 27

I just pictured in my mind what I wanted to do. You can use that same formula in accomplishing anything in life.

—IDA BELLEGARDE

The imagination is a powerful tool. With practice we can perfect our use of it and the results will astound us. Research has shown that athletes who visualize a practice session on the field or mountain or course hone their skills as effectively as those who practice "in the flesh." This may be hard to believe, but it's nonetheless true.

If this formula has worked for others, it can work for you too. But how do you begin? First, consider what you would like to do. The next step is to sit quietly, close your eyes and imagine, in detail, the activity you want to pursue. Stay quiet with this image until it feels natural. Take special note of the sensations you feel throughout your body, the colors you see around you, your inner voice's message. Absorb the experience fully before coming back to reality.

Repeated "journeys" with your mind will make any activity feel familiar, and enough familiarity makes success possible.

I am not prevented from doing anything I really want to do. Using my imagination to experience it the first time will get me started.

—from *Keepers of the Wisdom*

January 28

An artist is primarily one who has faith in himself.
—HENRY MILLER

"I'm not an artist," you might be saying. But there is another perspective: some would say we are all artists. Our accomplishments attest to that; our medium has simply differed. Another way of interpreting this message is that when we have faith in ourselves, we can create rich lives. The key, of course, is nurturing faith in ourselves. What are the steps to take?

Not everybody grew up with encouragement. We may have reached adulthood by the skin of our teeth. Having confidence in ourselves took effort and we often failed. But life is made up of effort and failure and more effort again.

Artists are many things, but first and foremost, they are comfortable in their daily activities, which may be at an easel, or in the kitchen, or in a classroom. It may be with others or alone. They seldom doubt what they can offer today. We are all artists. Just as surely as we are alive, we have a gift to offer others.

I will revel in my accomplishments today. My artistry has been revealed to others even though I may have failed to see it.

—from *Keepers of the Wisdom*

January 29

Harmony exists in difference no less than in likeness, if only the same key-note governs both parts.

—MARGARET FULLER

Harmony exists everywhere, as an entity of itself. Our personal attitudes bring the disharmony to a situation. An attitude of love can bless all situations and all people.

The converse is likewise true. We all desire harmony in our relationships. And we will find it, every time we bring an attitude of honest gratitude into a situation.

How we feel, today, about this person or that situation, reflects the strength of our relationship with God. When we experience life in the company of our higher power, we will let life flow. We will observe harmony, then, even in the midst of difference.

All of life's elements are moving toward a state of total and perfect harmony. We need not fear. We can trust the company of our higher power and know that every situation, no matter how adverse its appearance, is contributing to a harmonious outcome if we'd but lend a trusting attitude.

Harmony is everywhere. I will celebrate it. I will trust the present. I will trust the future.

—from *Each Day a New Beginning*

January 30

Practiced consistently, new habits become who I am.
—LIN ANDRUKAT

We sometimes have trouble defining ourselves. Anyone who spends much time in our presence, however, can define us pretty accurately. Our habits tell our "story" quite readily.

Many of our behaviors embarrass us, yet we repeat them. But changing them takes more than wishing they'd disappear. It takes a decision not to repeat them and the thoughtfulness to find a replacement for them. We return to hold behaviors more out of laziness than intent.

Those of us in a Twelve Step program have the tools to make this shift in our behavior easier. Doing a Fourth Step to look at the past, and frequent Tenth Steps to stay on top of today, gives us the insight to define who we are and who we'd rather be. Changing who we are isn't that difficult if we have the desire.

Any current behavior used to be "new." It became a habit only with continuous use. I can decide to begin a new behavior today.

—from *A Woman's Spirit*

January 31

A call for healing and help is easily recognized.

Any behavior we observe or are the brunt of can be classified instantly. It is either the reflection of a loving thought or an appeal for help and healing. Depending on its nature, the behavior triggers in us a response. Too often it will be ill-conceived. If we haven't consulted with the Holy Spirit first, we're letting the ego dictate our response, and the outcome benefits no one.

Isn't there a way to control our behavior? Certainly. And it's not a mystery known only to a few. We have been apprised of the presence of the Holy Spirit within our minds, but we may not have accessed it often. That's not unusual or something to be ashamed of. We're still learning. But we do need to acknowledge the truth of it, and then seek the Spirit's involvement in the preparation of all responses from this moment forth. When we do, no appeal for healing and help will be met with anger or worse.

I can be certain I'll hurt no one today if I consult with the Holy Spirit before taking action.

—from *Daily Meditations for Practicing the* Course

February

February 1

Do unto others . . .

Snapping at a friend often results in being snapped at in return. That doesn't surprise us. Accusations generally elicit an angry defense and an argument. That comes as no surprise either. By contrast, being loving and compassionate toward the people in our lives generally results in others returning love and compassion to us. Why, then, is it harder to express love?

The fear of rejection is strong for many of us. Offering love while fearing it won't be returned makes us feel too vulnerable. However, the principles we are being exposed to through this program will help us understand that we do receive from others what we give. The scales are balanced. Remembering that before responding to anyone around us will make our lives far more peaceful.

I will know what to expect from others today by how I treat them. I pray to be kind and loving.

—from *A Life of My Own*

February 2

Life is so much easier if we don't feel sorry for ourselves.

—HELEN CASEY

Our willingness to feel sorry for ourselves is related to our level of faith. When we cherish the knowledge that God has always been present, we can pull ourselves through any difficult experience. Some might say that our difficulties multiply as we age, and many situations are harder for us to handle. Perhaps we have less income and our bodies are less agile. But nothing has to get us down, and nothing will if we go to the ever-present Source for whatever we need.

When we decide to feel sorry for ourselves, we have effectively filled up our minds with thoughts that prevent us from hearing the inner voice of strength. If we listen to it instead, we'll not be overwhelmed by any situation that's happening. It might help to recall an earlier period in our lives when our faith walked us through a hard time. Perhaps we got fired or a marriage filled us with pain. When we sought comfort, it came to us. It still will. We need not feel abandoned, which is what we're feeling if trapped by self-pity. God didn't go anywhere. Only our minds left.

I will recall the Power of the Presence anytime I am scared or frustrated today. Comfort will come to call.

—from *Keepers of the Wisdom*

February 3

There is nothing else that can expand the human soul, actualize the human potential for growth, or bring a person into the full possession of life more than a love which is unconditional.

—JOHN POWELL, S.J.

A garden tended by loving hands reaps succulent fruits. Our attention to family and friends, when offered lovingly, likewise reaps rewards for all of us. Our efforts are not soon forgotten by us or our loved ones. Each loving act we express finds its home, in another's heart as well as our own.

The decision to love someone unconditionally is simply made—and yet it takes daily persistent effort. How quickly we forget the promised benefits. Each day a gentle reminder is needed.

"I will love wholly and nurture the fuller development of someone special." This one commitment, carried out, guarantees two vital, growing souls.

—from *Worthy of Love*

February 4

*We are empowered to decide exactly what kind of
day we will have, every day.*

So many times throughout the day we are inclined toward
anger, frustration, criticism, or perhaps all three. We love
to blame a situation or another person for how we are feeling. Many of us have shirked responsibility for our feelings
and our behavior.

When we came into the program and first learned that
we needed to be wholly accountable both for our feelings and for our behavior, we panicked. The responsibility
seemed overwhelming. On occasion, it still does. But it's
also exhilarating to know that we, and only we, can decide
how we are going to feel. No one can trigger behavior that
we aren't willing to display. No one can decide who we will
be or how we will feel; we are the ones in charge. That's a
wonderful gift.

*I am in charge of myself today. I'll enjoy my life, all of it, if I
choose to.*

—from *A Life of My Own*

February 5

What you desire with a burning desire, a continuing burning desire, you will draw to you.

—JEAN WILL

Our thoughts manifest themselves. That's both a powerful realization and a haunting one. Does it mean that we are to blame for the bad as well as the good experiences in our lives? Some wiser than ourselves would say yes. However, if our lives have been fraught with pain, that response doesn't comfort us. Let's settle, instead, for coming to believe that we have gotten what we needed for our growth, and it has taken many forms. We will continue to get whatever we need to make us whole.

Our journey has been full of surprises, right? Probably few of us imagined the turns our careers took. Nor did we anticipate the travels, the friends, the struggles in the midst of joys that our families experienced. And yet, all that we have come to know has benefited us. All that we have lived through enriched our contributions to others.

We may not be conscious of our souls' supreme desires. We must trust, however, that they have come to us in the right way at the right time. They will continue to do so.

My experiences have always been right for me. Even when I didn't like them, they were right. The same will be true today.

—from *Keepers of the Wisdom*

February 6

The bottom line is that I am responsible for my own well-being, my own happiness. The choices and decisions I make regarding my life directly influence the quality of my days.

—KATHLEEN ANDRUS

There is no provision for blaming others in our lives. Who we are is a composite of the actions, attitudes, choices, decisions we've made up to now. For many of us, predicaments may have resulted from our decisions to not act when the opportunity arose. But these were decisions, no less, and we must take responsibility for making them.

We need not feel utterly powerless and helpless about the events of our lives. True, we cannot control others, and we cannot curb the momentum of a situation, but we can choose our own responses to both; these choices will heighten our sense of self and well-being and may well positively influence the quality of the day.

I will accept responsibility for my actions, but not for the outcome of a situation; that is all that's requested of me. It is one of the assignments of life, and homework is forthcoming.

—from *Each Day a New Beginning*

February 7

The Holy Spirit is always present.

We can always count on the Holy Spirit to direct our thoughts and actions. However, we must be vigilant about asking for this guidance. We need to remember that the ego wants to be our director too. How do we know which "voice" we are listening to? The answer is always the same. If the act we are about to take or the words we are about to say are not purely loving, we aren't attuned to the Holy Spirit. It's just that simple.

Each day we are bombarded by opportunities to interact with other people who help us get in touch with our spiritual needs. Even the most difficult relationships offer us opportunities to grow and heal. Every person around us helps us return "home" to the realm of the Holy Spirit. In that realm, there is only love, nothing more. Our companions here, now, are the links to the realm of love.

I can have constant contact with the Holy Spirit if I am aware of the ego's attempts to control me.

—from *Daily Meditations for Practicing the* Course

February 8

Letting go of old hurts makes room for new joys.
—SEFRA KOBRIN PITZELE

Dwelling on the painful past gets tiresome eventually, but some of us hang on to it longer than others do. However, seeing women move from the bondage of the past to the freedom of living in the present gives us hope. Once we let go of the pain, we discover far more joy in even ordinary experiences. That's the real surprise.

We have heard sponsors say that when old doors close, new doors open. Letting go of old hurts in order to appreciate new joys falls into the same category. Why not fill our voids with joys rather than recollections of pain?

None of us know how long a life we'll be blessed with. Accepting how tentative life is helps us decide to seek more joy and less pain. The decision is only the first step, however. Taking control of how we think is the necessary action.

I will experience more joy if I give less thought to old hurts today. The decision is mine, and I can make it and remake it if necessary.

—from *A Woman's Spirit*

February 9

*The basis of happiness is the love of something
outside self.*

—WILLIAM GEORGE JORDON

Self-centeredness destroys the very self it purports to nurture. When our vision of an experience stops at the tips of our noses, we fail to notice the colorful passing panorama that promises the enlightenment for which we've been created. It's only through our interested involvement with others that we'll discover what we need to know. Perpetual introspection deprives us of the worldly information that nourishes each searching soul.

We lead muddled, directionless lives when we fail to listen to the clues for finding happiness being uttered by those we choose to ignore.

Just as we must water and thin our raspberries if they're to multiply, so must we cultivate the seeds of friendship if we're to know happiness. And attuning ourselves to the sounds of another's heart offers us a clearer perspective on our own.

—from *Worthy of Love*

February 10

What is not love is always fear.

We don't always interpret fear quickly. That's because it wears many faces. Violent rage seldom looks like fear to us. Neither does a bully's humiliation of a school chum. Tearful pleading may be recognized as fear, but only because it doesn't threaten us. Is every act that is not love fear? We may have to remind ourselves often that it is.

Daily we'll observe many instances of fear. The action called for from us is compassion. In the expression of it, we'll reap its benefit. In the same way that fear fosters more fear if not met with love, compassion also multiplies. Being a purveyor of the latter helps to heal all who enter our realm today.

Perhaps we think we can always recognize love, but is that true? Let's expand our horizons. Love may be silence. It may be laughter or tears. It may be unexpected agreement from an adversary. Love will never be hostile, but it may be subtle.

I will look for signs of love today. I will express them whether I see them or not.

—from *Daily Meditations for Practicing the* Course

February 11

*Our happiness doesn't depend on a loved
one's sobriety.*

What we do with our lives is not dependent on what others do with theirs. That's hard for us to believe, but we see how program friends have gone on with their dreams even though the drinker still drinks or the addict still snorts cocaine.

We come into the program expecting to learn how to help our loved ones stop using. That's our primary goal. What a jolt to discover that it hasn't happened for some who share our circle. And they come to meetings anyway. More than that, they seem to be leading happy lives. At first we wonder how.

We are guaranteed happiness too. We are enmeshed with our loved ones only because we have never understood separateness. Our boundaries have been blurred. But the guidance of sponsors and the wisdom we'll gain from the meetings will show us how to disengage from others. Our first step toward the happiness we're promised is to give up our attempts to control anyone but ourselves.

I have my own dreams, my own goals. To fulfill them, I must turn my attention away from others and on to me. I can't make anyone else's life my dream.

—from *A Life of My Own*

February 12

You start preparing when you're thirty for the person you'll be at eighty.

—JANICE CLARK

We can't get away from ourselves, at least not entirely. Who we were at ten and twenty and forty and fifty remains as threads in our tapestries. Many of us shudder because some details of our personal panorama weren't so very pretty. But that's the way life is. We are what we are. And yet, we have examples of favorable changes, too. How we were never kept us from becoming who we wanted to be. This truth continues to reign in our lives.

We all know women and men who continue to be enthused about even the tiny happenings in the passing of a day. A bird's flight from the porch to a nearby tree to feed its young, the laughter of children passing the house on their way home from school, the family reunions, large or small, bring smiles and memories that comfort. Probably we envy those folks, unless we happen to be *them* already. In either case, imitating others or serving as their role models helps to strengthen our positive responses to life's details. No matter how old we are, there is still joy to be felt. And there is still time to change and grow.

There is no rule that says I have to be and think and act the same way my whole life. Today is a clean slate. I can be who I want to be.

—from *Keepers of the Wisdom*

February 13

. . . *the growth of understanding follows an ascending spiral rather than a straight line.*

—JOANNA FIELD

We each are traveling our own, very special path in this life. At times our paths run parallel to each other. On occasion they may intersect. But we do all have a common destination: knowledge of life's meaning. And we'll arrive at knowledge when we've arrived at the mountain's summit separately and yet together.

We do not go straight up the side of the mountain on this trip. We circle it, slowly, carefully, sometimes losing our footing, sometimes backtracking because we've reached an impasse. Many times we have stumbled, but as we grow in understanding, as we rely more and more on our inner strength, available for the taking, we become more sure-footed.

We have never needed to take any step alone on this trip. Our troubles in the past were complicated because we did not know this; but now we do. Our lifeline is to our higher power. If we hang on to it, every step of the way will feel secure. The ground will be stable under us.

I am on a path to full understanding. I am learning to trust the lifeline offered by the program and God and my friends. As I learn, my footing is less tentative, and it supports me more securely.

—from *Each Day a New Beginning*

February 14

*Our behavior won't be irrational if we pause and
think before acting.*

Reacting to another person's craziness makes us a bit
crazy too. However, someone else's anger, even if directed
at us, doesn't have to trigger our anger in return.

All it takes to stop our troubling behavior is the willingness to be quiet a moment so we can think clearly before
taking action. That sounds simple enough. Surely we can
do it. But it takes practice, lots of it. Most of us have spent
years reacting without thinking and then blaming the
messy outcome on the other guy. At first, doing it the new
way won't feel familiar, so our tendency will be to revert to
the old behavior. Looking to the people we admire in the
program for help will give us the inspiration to keep trying.

*I will become adept at thinking before acting. Today will give me
many opportunities to succeed.*

—from *A Life of My Own*

February 15

What thoughts are you willing to give up your happiness for?

—JANE NELSON

Far too quickly we put the responsibility for our happiness on others. We pout and blame and cry, but our lives never change. This doesn't have to be true, however. We can decide to follow the example of the happier women we are discovering in this Twelve Step program. The difference between them and us is their willingness to be responsible for every thought they have, every feeling they harbor. It's a simple change in mind-set, but it affects every aspect of their lives.

We are just as capable of finding happiness as any of the women we have grown to admire here. They have taken back their power from the others in their lives. They let no one decide how they are going to feel or think about a situation. They take charge of themselves. It's not all that difficult or there would be far fewer successes. Let's try it today.

I can purposefully decide how I'll think and feel today. No one else's behavior will control my own.

—from *A Woman's Spirit*

February 16

Our relationships always reflect our state of mind.

Sometimes we feel hurt and angry at everyone. It seems as if the world is out to get us. At those times, it's well to remember that our attitudes deeply influence how we see the world and the people around us. We can remember to "turn the other cheek." When we meet an affront with kindness, the perpetrator miraculously backs off. The lesson is not that elusive.

We frequently lament the characteristics of our relationships. There is not enough intimacy, there is too much disagreement, or we share too few interests. Perhaps we have too few friends. The solution to our relationship problems is to check out our inner perceptions. The signals we send to others define what we get back in return.

When we meet happy people, we'll likely soon see the balance in their lives, the level of peace in their relationships. Positive attitudes and healthy relationships go hand in hand. Fortunately, we're in charge of the attitudes we nurture.

I am seeking the hand of the Holy Spirit today. The joy is mine.

—from *Daily Meditations for Practicing the* Course

February 17

❧

To show great love for God and our neighbor, we need not do great things.

—MOTHER TERESA

We don't have to invent a cure for cancer or lift the burdens of a friend to prove our worth to other people. Being considerate of someone's feelings is quite enough, and it is something any of us can do. It takes only a moment's thought and the willingness to treat others as we'd like them to treat us. The real blessing is that we feel much better each time our heart guides our actions.

Loving others is perhaps the simplest of all actions we can take in this life. It requires no planning, no money, no muscle power, no problem solving. It's a simple decision we can make daily or hourly. Every person we encounter, every situation we face, is an opportunity for us to hone the skill. And every loving act or thought makes the world a better place.

It's human nature to treat others as we are treated. If each of us becomes willing to offer the hand of love to someone else today, we will indeed have done a great thing!

I can make a worthwhile contribution today. I can be kind to a stranger.

—from *A Woman's Spirit*

February 18

Believing in a Higher Power changes our perspective.

Gone are the long days of feeling adrift, days we had no hope or direction. For too long we agonized over the circumstances of our lives, tormented by the drinking and lying of our loved ones. Our attempts to control didn't work. They still won't. Yet some days we try anyway.

Most days, though, we use the principles of the program, relying on the wisdom of the first three Steps to take our focus off the person we're trying to control. Accepting that we are powerless, coming to believe in a Power that is greater than we are, letting it guide the behavior of the other person and ourselves—these things give us clarity and peace about the actions we need to make. We aren't adrift today.

I am so lucky that I have a greater Power that I can call on today. I can be certain that I'll be taken care of.

—from *A Life of My Own*

February 19

If a man can carve something out of wood, he is just as much a creator as a man who works with words.
—CLARA GLENN

It's really not *what* we do in life that matters, but *how* we do it. To more clearly understand this, let's take an example. We can all remember dreading a project that needed doing—maybe mending some pants or replacing a screen in the back door. First, we couldn't find our glasses to thread the needle, then we stuck ourselves with the needle, drawing blood that promptly got on the pants. Or we hit our index finger with the hammer as we attempted to install the new screen. Our recollections are endless. Interestingly enough, our personal attitudes always directly controlled the success we had with the project.

What does this mean to us now? It suggests that if we are fully attentive to whatever we pursue, our experience of it will be significantly different. We are competent to handle anything that needs our attention. In most cases, we'll be more than competent. And if we have a real desire to do the job, we'll excel at it, providing we give it our undivided attention.

I am a creator of something today. Maybe it's a friendship or a poem. They are equal in the eyes of God.

—from *Keepers of the Wisdom*

February 20

Imagination has always had powers of resurrection
that no science can match.

—INGRID BENGIS

In the imagination are transmitted messages, from God to us. Inspiration is born there. So are dreams. Both give rise to the goals that urge us forward, that invite us to honor this life we've been given with a contribution, one like no other contribution.

Our imagination offers us ideas to ponder, ideas specific to our development. It encourages us to take steps unique to our time, our place, our intended gifts to the world. We can be alert to this special "inner voice" and let it guide our decisions; we can trust its urgings. It's charged with serving us, but only we can decide to "listen."

The imagination gives us another tool: belief in ourselves. And the magic of believing offers us strength and capabilities even beyond our fondest hopes. It prepares us for the effort we need to make and for handling whatever outcome God has intended.

My imagination will serve me today. It will offer me the ideas and the courage I need to go forth.

—from *Each Day a New Beginning*

February 21

Change the mind and the behavior follows.

Not one of us feels loving every minute. Even when we have been students of the *Course* for a long time, we are prone to behavior that embarrasses us at times. Why can't we change, once and for all? Actually, we can. That's the path we are on. We simply haven't arrived at the destination yet. In the meantime, we can take every chance we get to change our thoughts of attack to thoughts of love or forgiveness.

In some situations, it seems easier to change our behavior than our minds. For instance, when arguing with a friend, we may be certain we are right. But we don't have to yell or pout. We may keep our opinion, in fact, and our friends can keep theirs. It doesn't matter really. And that's what we come to understand. None of these differences really matter. They are nothing more than vehicles for learning what is real, what is important.

The quiet mind knows the only truth that matters. We will visit that place more frequently now. Our behavior will signal the change in us.

I may hope to change someone else by my actions today. That's folly. All I can change is my mind and my desire to change other people.

—from *Daily Meditations for Practicing the* Course

February 22

We need to share our problems to find our solutions.

Trying to solve a problem alone, without the benefit of the wisdom of other people, often leaves us stuck with an even worse problem. On the other hand, sharing any problem with interested, compassionate people, such as those we meet in the program, guarantees that many responses will surface. Each person will offer a unique and genuine perspective from which the best solution can be gleaned.

It's not unusual that we kept our problems to ourselves for years. Most of us were ashamed that we didn't have perfect lives; we thought most of the people we knew did. We didn't know that our secrets kept us very stuck. Now we are learning that sharing secrets with trusted others frees us from the burden of our secrets. We can make progress toward those perfect lives only if we tell who we really are and what is really going on. What surprises have been in store for us since we joined the program!

Telling a trusted friend about a problem will make this day more productive. And the problem may get solved too!

—from *A Life of My Own*

February 23

Life does not need to mutilate itself in order to
be pure.

—SIMONE WEIL

How terribly complicated we choose to make life's many
questions. Should we call a friend and apologize or wait
for her call? Are the children getting the kind of care they
must, right now? That we "Came to believe in a power
greater than ourselves" is often far from our thoughts
when we most need it.

Our need to make all things perfect, to know all the
answers, to control everything within our range, creates
problems where none really exist. And the more we focus
on the problem we've created, the bigger it becomes.

Inattention relieves the tension; last week's problems
can seldom be recalled. The one we are keeping a problem
with our undivided attention can be turned loose, at this
moment. And just as quickly, the turmoil we've been feeling will be beyond recall too.

The program offers us another way to approach life. We
need not mutilate it or ourselves. We can learn to accept
the things we cannot change, and change the things we
can . . . with practice.

I will pray for wisdom today. I shall expect wisdom, not problems,
and the day will smoothly slip by.

—from Each Day a New Beginning

February 24

Perception is not a fact.

Thousands of arguments might have been avoided had we known the meaning of *perception*. What we saw seemed real or true, and when others observed the same situation, it seemed sensible to assume that how we saw it was the right way. But now all that's changed, and the impact of this new information has changed our lives forever.

The *Course* informs us that *what* we perceive depends on *who* we put in charge of perception. The ego's watchful eye perceives a darker picture than does the Spirit. When two people are present, both may see through their ego lens. Confusion occurs. Argument results. And the true picture is missed by both.

But what is the true picture? We will always see it when we shed the light of the Holy Spirit on it. The details are never important. The underlying message is always the same: Forgive and feel love and you will feel peaceful.

I'll perceive peace and joy if I look through God's eyes today.

—from *Daily Meditations from Practicing the* Course

February 25

I guess all work is leisure time to me.
—VIOLET HENSLEY

The attitude a person cultivates is solely an individual matter. Money doesn't determine it. We have all known wealthy, resentful people. Health doesn't determine it either. Nary a one of us hasn't met a disabled man or woman who still encounters the day wearing a smile. Deciding to feel blessed, thus content with life, comes from our interior spaces. We do reflect to others whatever we feel within.

What kind of people are we? The good news is that whoever we have been doesn't need to limit us anymore. We aren't committed to being depressed or fearful or angry unless we have given our power over to that emotion. And even if we have, we can take it back and be serene and hopeful instead.

I am in charge of my perspective today, like every day. Beginning with a prayer for peace will help me attain it.

—from *Keepers of the Wisdom*

February 26

God is the only constant.

—RUTH CASEY

Change is happening to us every minute. Scientists tell us that all our body's cells are replaced every few months. We are losing old hair and growing new hair every day. The plant world participates in a cycle of death and renewal every minute. We are surrounded by change. And when it's change that doesn't affect our egos, we accept it without comment, or in many cases, without notice.

Change in our personal lives is not so easily accepted. Losing a job can be devastating. Ending a relationship might feel unsurvivable. Moving to a new community, away from friends, can be profoundly lonely and disorienting. We haven't been promised unchanging lives. But we have been promised an unchanging, always-loving Higher Power. The most fruitful lessons we can learn are that God is with us throughout every experience and that change is introduced in our lives only when it helps us fulfill our greater purpose.

I will trust the experiences in store for me today and have faith they are part of God's plan.

—from *A Woman's Spirit*

February 27

Love, the magician, knows this little trick whereby
two people walk in different directions yet always
remain side by side.

—HUGH PRATHER

Destiny has its own course in each of our lives. And our
movements with others who are special will thankfully be
parallel at times. However, our paths will sharply intersect
now and then and we'll even find ourselves at painful
cross-purposes on occasion. But if the love we're expressing is part of God's plan for us and not just to satisfy the
selfish ego, we'll not stray from one another's dream,
though we may depart for brief periods of new growth.

We must fulfill our personal desires, vocationally and
recreationally, if we are to successfully offer up our special
talents for the goodness of humankind. And most assuredly that's why we're here—in this place—at this time—
with these particular people.

Others cannot pull us from our true calling. If the love
between us is real, it will free us and bless our direction—
trusting our hearts will not be torn asunder.

The butterfly silently returns when the winds blow free.

—from *Worthy of Love*

February 28

To see imperfectly is not to see at all.

Our judgment of others comes from not seeing them as they really are. What we see mirrors our own imperfections. If we honored our own perfection, we'd see only perfection in others. What we think we are, we see. What we receive from others, we expect.

Upon awakening, we may look in the mirror and see a body we don't like. Our dismay lingers as we prepare for work. We think about the day ahead and our mind wanders to a contentious co-worker. Unfortunately, these thoughts may make us feel slightly superior; however, we have seen neither the co-worker nor ourselves as we really are.

Do we want to see what's really there? If so, we must ask for the better, true view, first of ourselves, and then of everyone else. If we're mindful about doing this, we'll begin to experience a very different world.

I look but don't really see. I will alter my view today.

—from *Daily Meditations for Practicing the* Course

February 29

We grow in darkness and in light.
—MARILYN MASON

Every experience is a learning opportunity. The abuse we suffered, whether physical or emotional, taught us survival and resilience. Even though we felt defeated, we are here now, and we've learned to recognize relationships that aren't good for us. That's evidence of growth.

Sponsors tell us we are always growing. Even when it feels like we are going backward, we are growing. Recognizing our slower pace signals our awareness, and that is growth too.

Gone are the days when we doubted our ability to grow, to change. One of the first lessons we learn in recovery is that change is possible. Every meeting surrounds us with examples. And much of the growth has come through the dark periods of our lives. The darkness and the light have much to teach us. Every moment is to be revered for its message.

I am ready to grow today. Regardless of the kind of experience I'm having, I'll realize its worth to me.

—from *A Woman's Spirit*

March

March 1

*I think everybody has to experience a certain
amount of pain on the way to maturity.*
—RUTH CASEY

Our lives have been a series of lessons, many of them not particularly easy. It's generally the case that the ones we gained the most from were the hardest or the most tedious. Is pain always a requirement for growth? Hindsight may suggest that, but we need to realize that our willingness to grow or change, coupled with the faith that we were always in safe hands, could have made all of our transitions quite smooth. Nothing ever had to be as hard as some of us made it.

Attitude, along with faith, has always had a powerful impact on our perceptions of life. No two people have ever made identical observations of any situation. Needless to say, we all make a choice about how to interpret the varied circumstances in our life. So-called accidents of nature are seen as quite purposeful to some, while others are defeated by them. Physical ailments are accepted as opportunities for developing another dimension of one's life by those who prefer a positive outlook. Our freedom to interpret each experience as a lucky opportunity or as undeserved devastation has always existed and will never be taken from us. How have we managed that power so far?

Am I content with how my life has evolved? Where it goes today is in my power.

—from *Keepers of the Wisdom*

March 2

Today was like a shadow. It lurked behind me.
It's now gone forever. Why is it that time is such
a difficult thing to befriend?

—MARY CASEY

Each passing minute is all that we are certain of having. The choice is ever present to relish the moment, reaping fully whatever its benefits, knowing that we are being given just what we need each day of our lives. We must not pass up what is offered today.

Time accompanies us like a friend, though often a friend denied or ignored. We can't recapture what was offered yesterday. It's gone. All that stands before us is here, now.

We can nurture the moment and know that the pain and pleasures offered us with each moment are our friends, the teachers our inner selves await. And we can be mindful that this time, this combination of events and people, won't come again. They are the gift of the present. We can be grateful.

We miss the opportunities the day offers because we don't recognize the experiences as the lesson designed for the next stage of our development. The moment's offerings are just, necessary, and friendly to our spiritual growth.

I will take today in my arms and love it. I will love all it offers; it is a friend bearing gifts galore.

—from *Each Day a New Beginning*

March 3

*Accepting that we are powerless seems difficult
at first.*

We have felt responsible for so many people for so long
that giving up our control scares us. What will *they* do?
Perhaps the more important question is, what will *we* do?
Where do we put our focus when we no longer put it on
others?

We probably didn't understand the meaning or the
value of the Serenity Prayer when we were first introduced
to it. We had spent most of our lives forcing change, or at
least trying to. Accepting conditions or the people we
loved as they were was beyond our comprehension. After
all, wouldn't they want to change if they could see themselves as we saw them?

Now we are coming to understand our powerlessness.
The glimpses we get no longer scare us. Not being in charge
of others anymore also means we are not to blame for their
shortcomings. And that part of powerlessness we like.

*I will enjoy my powerlessness today. "Giving up" the behavior of
others will lighten my own load considerably.*

—from *A Life of My Own*

March 4

*We're not going to live forever, but I think we should
have the attitude of "Why not?"*
                              —HARRY BARTHOLOMEW

Taking our focus off of the future and placing it instead
on whatever presents itself today adds a richness to each
moment that can't be measured or duplicated. Dwelling
on our deaths or the ill health that might befall us leaves
us no free time to laugh and learn from all the experiences
that are presenting themselves. The end will come. Of that
we can be sure, but why let thinking about it *discolor* every
minute that remains between now and then?

Most of us have no idea what our real purpose has been
in this life, in these bodies. It's quite freeing to give up the
need to know why we're here. It's far more fascinating to
simply acknowledge that we are here, and the friends and
strangers who walk with us are all that matter minute by
minute. Figuring out nothing more than this lets us give
our total being over to whatever experience has called to
us, as though it's all there ever was or ever will be. Nothing
appears the same, from the past or the present, when we
see it this way.

I have all the time I need to do whatever comes to me today.

—from *Keepers of the Wisdom*

March 5

~o~

Accepting powerlessness lightens our burdens.

Coming to believe that we are not responsible for solving anyone else's problems or making anyone else's decisions frees us to pursue our own dreams and aspirations with greater concentration. But it's not easy to give up our control of other people. It's how we thought we were supposed to live. Their burdens had become ours.

We surely have lots more time to take care of ourselves now that we have begun letting others be in charge of themselves. But we have to watch out for slipping back into our old controlling behaviors. Ingrained habits are hard to change. We have to learn how to savor the extra hours in our day now that we only have ourselves to control. As our accomplishments multiply, we'll find that letting others take care of themselves will be easier.

I am in charge of myself. What do I want to accomplish? I can begin right away.

—from *A Life of My Own*

March 6

In soloing—as in other activities—it is far easier to
start something than it is to finish it.

—AMELIA EARHART

Procrastination plagues us all, at one time or another. But
any activity that is worthy of our effort should be tackled
by bits and pieces, one day at a time. We are too easily overwhelmed when we set our sights only on the accomplished
goal. We need to focus, instead, on the individual elements
and then on just one element at a time. A book is written,
word by word. A house is built, timber by timber. A college
degree is attained, course by course.

By the time we got to this program, most of us had accumulated a checkered past, much of which we wanted to
deny or forget. And the weight of our past can stand in the
way of the many possibilities in the present.

Our past need not determine what we set out to do
today. However, we must be realistic: We can't change a behavior pattern overnight. But we can begin the process. We
can decide on a reasonable, manageable objective for this
24-hour period. Enough days committed to the completion of enough small objectives will bring us to the attainment of any goal, large or small.

*I can finish any task I set my sights on, when I take it one day at a
time. Today is before me. I can move forward in a small way.*

—from *Each Day a New Beginning*

March 7

❧

Something needs to be done in the course of a day.
—EDITH SHANNON

Where did we learn to be productive? Perhaps from parents who expected chores to be done. Or maybe from the popular refrain heard in every classroom by every child: "Get busy!" The stories we read as children usually lauded the fruits of being industrious. The message was everywhere. And nothing has changed.

Being productive isn't a failing. In fact, without committing to productivity we'd never have attained any goal we set for ourselves. Our past accomplishments wouldn't have materialized. But a lesson we deserve to learn—and it's never too late—is that we can define "getting something done" as loosely and as imaginatively as we wish. This is surely one of the rewards of old age.

Feeling as though we have made a difference is what we really yearn for. How we make that difference is as varied and optional as our minds can fathom.

Something as simple as smiling at a stranger is getting something done. I can brighten someone's world so easily today.

—from *Keepers of the Wisdom*

March 8

All problems can be handled by changing our minds
about them.

For most of us it's a radical opinion, at least initially, to believe that our problems can be relinquished at will. After
all, they seem so integral to all the experiences we're having. Indeed they are; however, our experiences mirror our
thoughts about ourselves and the people we're with. Problems thus lie with our perceptions.

Being told that we can change our lives by changing our
minds seems simplistic. The events that involve us appear
far too complicated for such an easy solution. But until we
earnestly try to change our minds, we'll not understand
the power we garner at the blink of an eye. The Holy Spirit
is just as accessible as the ego. If we want to see something,
in fact anything, differently, all we need to do is ask the
Holy Spirit for a better vision of the circumstance. One
will come to us.

Today I choose to change my mind about problems.

—from *Daily Meditations for Practicing the* Course

March 9

Ideally, both members of a couple in love free each other to new and different worlds.
—ANNE MORROW LINDBERGH

We cannot possess another's spirit, even though we may desire to do so while struggling to feel love. We must not block one another's invitations for adventure even though we fear being left behind. We won't find the happiness we long for if we've tied another to ourselves by strings of shame, guilt, or pity.

Being free to love, or not, is the only path to real love. A trapped butterfly soon loses its splendor, and life; likewise, a trapped lover quietly awaits the relationship's death.

Traveling separate, yet parallel, paths keeps a relationship vital. Bringing fresh ideas, favored hopes, and fruitful experiences to each other's attention is the enhancement a relationship must have to stay strong.

Let's not corner our patterns but instead trust that real love is the promised gift of being free.

—from *Worthy of Love*

March 10

*Everything passes, and as I flow with this river
of highs and lows, I become calm. I trust my
experience and the life force guiding me.*

—RUTHIE ALBERT

Everything passes. There is perhaps no greater comfort
when we're caught in the throes of trauma than the knowledge that this too shall pass. We lived many years without
this knowledge as we struggled to change the unchange-
able. Unfortunately, the only thing that changed was our
level of frustration: it got higher. Now we know that we
can patiently wait for a situation to pass. Nothing lasts
forever.

The good times pass too, of course. We hope to hold on
to them, but the same principle applies. The minutes tick
by, carrying us to new experiences. What we need to learn
will become known to us through both the good times
and the struggles. They all will pass, having prepared us
for the highs and lows that wait to serve us.

*I am at peace with the knowledge that everything passes. My needs
will be met today.*

—from *A Woman's Spirit*

March 11

*Pity is the deadliest feeling that can be offered to
a woman.*

—VICKI BAUM

We must move forward with confidence, trusting that the strength we need will be given us, having faith in our visions to guide us. Problems need not daunt us. Rather, they can spur us on to more creative activity. They challenge our capabilities. They insist that we not stand still.

Pity from others fosters inaction, and passivity invites death of the soul. Instead, our will to live is quickened through others' encouragement. All else dampens the will. Pity feeds the self-pity that rings the death knell.

We can give strokes wherever we are today and know that we are helping someone live. And each time we reach out to encourage another, we are breathing new life into ourselves, new life that holds at bay the self-pity that may appear at any moment.

We can serve one another best, never by commiserating with sadnesses, but by celebrating life's challenges. They offer the opportunities necessary to our continued growth.

Someone needs a word of encouragement from me. I will brighten her vision of the future.

—from Each Day a New Beginning

March 12

Every event is an opportunity for healing and forgiving.

The *Course* tells us that we are here, in this realm, to heal. The people we encounter, the experiences we love and abhor, the dreams that scare or tantalize us—these are not coincidental. We have sought them for the growth we deserve and desire. Along the journey we'll meet "ourselves" repeatedly and every encounter offers us the chance for self-awareness and self-forgiveness.

Some of us will take far longer to heal than others. Our willingness to acknowledge that our reactions to others are mere reflections of ourselves quickens the journey. Our resistance does quite the opposite. How we hate to admit that what bothers us in another reflects our own shortcomings.

Forgiving others mysteriously lessens our own self-condemnation. In time, we realize this is the paramount lesson in our entire journey.

Today promises me experiences to practice forgiveness. Each time I do, I'll heal a little bit more.

—from *Daily Meditations for Practicing the* Course

March 13

❧

We can know the difference between God's will and our will.

The Third Step suggests that we turn our will over to God. That's a stumbling block for many of us. We don't know how to do it, and it's not easy for our friends in the program to explain the process. With patience, though, we come to realize it's more a feeling than anything else.

Pushing our will on someone else results in conflict and tension. We can learn to recognize negative feelings as signs that we're not doing God's will. Becoming willing to pause long enough to ask ourselves what God would want us to do in a specific situation, and then doing it, assures us that God's will, not our will, is in charge. We'll then feel peace.

Recovery is showing us the difference between peace and tension, God's will and our will. Willingness to try a better way to live with others guarantees that we'll recognize God's will every moment, if that's our desire.

I want to feel peaceful today. Asking for knowledge of God's will and then following it will make me peaceful.

—from *A Life of My Own*

March 14

People do need to have a purpose, some direction in life, both before and after retirement.

—LOUISE JEROME

Getting up every morning is far more exciting when we can anticipate being engaged with people or activities that interest us. Mattering to the world around us is important. Even when we aren't consciously aware of it, we matter to everyone we come into contact with. This has always been true and nothing has changed.

While still occupied in a profession or as a homemaker we didn't often doubt that we had a purpose. We had a place to be every day and tasks to be completed. We might not have considered that what we did made much of a contribution to the greater world, but we knew it counted, nonetheless. It's not as easy to believe this now. Maybe that's because we aren't currently involved in any specific activities that touch other people. But few days pass that we don't have contact with at least one other person. Quite possibly, that's the only purpose we have right now: being present to that one individual, whoever he or she might be.

Our purpose need not be *grand* to be important. God has need of each one of us. We are still needed, absolutely. All we have to do is "report for duty." We do that by awaking each morning.

I look to today with anticipation. God has a job for me and I'm ready.

—from *Keepers of the Wisdom*

March 15

Love one another, but make not a bond of love.
—KAHLIL GIBRAN

Love doesn't demand; love compromises. It doesn't possess; it frees. Love doesn't gloat; it praises. Love makes friends of strangers. It softens our rough edges and strengthens our assets. Knowing we're loved inspires us and invites forth our best effort. Offering our love humbles us and cultivates an inner joy.

Never, in the name of love, should we direct another person's life, but instead let's celebrate the choices made by someone dear, even when they run counter to our own desires. We are each blessed with a destiny, unique and necessary to the others in our lives. We must be allowed to travel our paths to fulfillment. Let's free one another and know real love.

—from *Worthy of Love*

March 16

*We're all recovering, all the time, from something;
we're growing out of the old and into the new.*

— JAN LLOYD

We are in a constant state of change. With each passing moment we are gathering new insights, collecting new experiences, defining new perspectives. Even when it feels as if our friends are passing us by, we can take comfort in knowing that we are not standing still.

The rate of growth is different for each of us. It depends on how quickly we assimilate the growth experiences and specific information our Higher Power wills for us. The more we struggle against the closing of a familiar passageway and the opening of a new door, the more our pace is hindered. We can quicken the pace by trusting that we are always given exactly what our Higher Power has in mind for our next stage of living.

Each day's experiences are part of the trip that God has planned for us. We will never be in danger as long as we trust the spiritual guidance that speaks to us in the quiet places of our minds.

I am in safe hands. I can leave the old behind and trust the growth experiences I will receive today.

—from *A Woman's Spirit*

March 17

*It isn't for the moment you are struck that you need
courage, but for the long uphill climb back to sanity
and faith and security.*

—ANNE MORROW LINDBERGH

Most of us are on a long uphill climb at this moment. It is
a climb we are making together, and yet a climb we can't
do for each other. I can reach out my hand to you, and you
can grasp my hand in return. But my steps are my own,
just as you, too, can only take one step at a time.

For brief periods we skip, even run, along the uphill
path. The rocks and the occasional boulder momentarily
trip us up. We need patience and trust that the summit is
still achievable. We can help one another have patience. We
can remind one another to trust.

We look back at the periods that devastated us so long
ago. And now we are here. We have climbed this far. We
are stronger, saner, more secure. Each step makes easier
the next step—each step puts us on more solid ground.

*I may run into some rocks or even a boulder today. I have stepped
around them in the past. I will do so again.*

—from *Each Day a New Beginning*

March 18

Turning the other cheek doesn't mean giving up our right to respond.

Revenge is not an option once we get accustomed to the Twelve Step principles. It never did give us more than a short-term rush, and it usually left us with guilt—lots of it. Now we are learning to acknowledge the boundaries between us and other people. This helps us detach from their mean-spiritedness, which often has prompted our own vengeful behavior.

It's important to distinguish between letting others stomp on us and letting them have their behavior. The program doesn't say we should take abuse; it suggests instead that we rationally tailor our response, relying on God as our speechwriter. If we respond calmly and firmly, without attacking, we give all concerned an opportunity to calm down.

Far fewer will be the times we're haunted by guilt if we follow this action plan. Acting responsibly, with God's help, will feel right and honorable to ourselves and the "opposition."

I need to stand up for myself always and, just as important, rely on God for support.

—from *A Life of My Own*

March 19

We didn't have any money growing up, but that isn't the essential. We had happiness.

—HELEN CASEY

One of the most important lessons in life is how "value-less" money really is. While it's true, we need enough to take care of our physical needs; more than that brings little additional benefit. There are literally millions of wealthy, unhappy people in this world. It's trite and profoundly true that money doesn't buy happiness.

Where does happiness come from? Let's take a brief inventory of the times we have laughed in the past week. Were we opening envelopes containing money? That, of itself, is laughable. But the point is that happiness resides in our minds, not in other people, in possessions, or in wishes. We make it ourselves. We know this, certainly. But we forget it just as certainly.

The benefit of remembering this is that each day can be as much fun as we decide to make it. Being old or infirm or poor doesn't demand that we be unhappy too. What a powerful idea this is. And it's available to us every minute.

I am in charge of the kind of day I'll have today. This has always been true, but I'll respect that thought today!

—from *Keepers of the Wisdom*

March 20

Healing our minds is our purpose.

Sometimes we forget just how elementary our assignment on this journey is. It's all about changing our minds. We're actually familiar with changing our minds. We have done it repeatedly throughout our lives. We've changed our minds about friends, neighbors, jobs, spouses. The style of clothes, cars, or houses that appealed to us changed over time. How we've spent our leisure time has changed many times too. So what's the big deal about changing our minds?

This *change of mind* changes everything about our lives. We will see every instance in time differently than ever before. Seeing each person and every event with loving and forgiving eyes allows us to see them as never before. No matter how many times we've looked at a friend or lover, we have not seen that person as we will from now on. Healing our minds is changing them. The miracles will follow.

Asking the Holy Spirit for a change of mind is my only task today.

—from *Daily Meditations for Practicing the* Course

March 21

Life is like an unbridled horse.
—KAY LOVATT

Many of us thought we knew where we were going after we finished school. We selected a path that fit our personality, we thought. Motherhood, a career, or both. Perhaps a single life or a low-stress job. Our friends suited our choices. So did our homes, our hobbies, our dreams. But then something happened. We didn't plan on addiction. Our drinking or drug use seemed social, at least initially. Where did the path veer? Why didn't we see the changes in store?

Life is full of surprises. Many are unwanted at first. But if we're willing to accept them as opportunities, we can discover greater meaning for our lives. Twelve Step recovery is one of those opportunities. Many new changes are in store. We may no longer know where we're going, but we will get to where we need to be. Let's hang on and enjoy the ride.

I am on the right course even if I don't know exactly where it leads. I will let my trusted friends take the lead today.

—from *A Woman's Spirit*

March 22

It is only with the heart that one can see rightly . . . .
—ANTOINE DE SAINT EXUPERY

If we look at the world through suspicious or angry eyes, we'll find a world that mirrors our expectations—a world where tension will mount, arguments will abound, strife will be present where none need be. However, our experiences in some manner bless us, and we'll recognize that if we'll look upon them with gratitude. Everything in our path is meant for our good and we'll see the good when our hearts act as the eyes for our minds.

When we see with our hearts, our responses to the turmoil around us, the fighting children, the traffic snarls, the angry lovers, will be soft acceptance. When our hearts guide the action we can accept those things we cannot change, and change those we can. And the heart, as the seat of all wisdom, will always know the difference.

—from *Worthy of Love*

March 23

No person is your enemy, no person is your friend,
every person is your teacher.

—FLORENCE SCOVEL SHINN

We can open ourselves to opportunities today. They abound in our lives. No circumstance we find ourselves in is detrimental to our progress. No relationship with someone at work or at home is superfluous to our development. Teachers are everywhere. And as we become ready for a new lesson, one will appear.

We can marvel at the wonder of our lives today. We can reflect on our yesterdays and be grateful for the lessons they taught. We can look with hopeful anticipation at the days ahead—gifts, all of them. We are on a special journey, serving a special purpose, uniquely our own. No barrier, no difficult person, no tumultuous time is designed to interrupt our progress. All experiences are simply to teach us what we have yet to learn.

Trusting in the goodness of all people, all situations, all paths to progress will release whatever our fears, freeing us to go forth with a quicker step and an assurance that eases all moments.

The Twelve Steps help us to recognize the teachers in our lives. They help us clear away the baggage of the past and free us to accept and trust the will of God, made known to us by the teachers as they appear.

I am a student of life. I can learn only if I open my mind to my teachers.

—from *Each Day a New Beginning*

March 24

Miracles aren't reserved for the few.

The *Course* is perhaps the only source of teaching which lets us know that miracles are available to all of us. What we're learning here is that miracles aren't as mysterious as we'd believed. You don't have to be anyone but who you are to receive one. In fact, you can claim one for yourself at any time you choose.

To receive a miracle takes no more time than an instant. It doesn't take a special prayer, a unique relationship with God, or an extremely unfortunate life. It takes only an open mind and a willing heart.

But what's the process for receiving a miracle? It's asking a simple question. "Holy Spirit, will you please help me see this situation in a more loving way?" *Miraculously,* the new perspective comes. *Miraculously,* the burden of worry or fear or anger dissolves.

A miracle is reserved for me today if I want it.

—from *Daily Meditations for Practicing the* Course

March 25

❧

"God, grant me the serenity . . ."

The Serenity Prayer has the potential of changing our lives concretely. The hardest part is remembering to rely on it. What the prayer offers is an opportunity to quiet our minds long enough to sense what our Higher Power wishes for us. In the stillness, we'll find the courage to accept what we must and the strength to change what we need to change.

It's not unusual to think that everyone but us needs to change. Ask around at meetings. All will agree that we came to our first meeting thinking we'd learn how to get other people to change, certain that would make us happy. But that's not how happiness comes, and we're lucky for that. If our happiness were tied to what others did, we'd always be in their control. What a bleak existence that might be!

The happiness we deserve will come when we do two things: first, take the power that is ours through becoming willing to accept others as they are; and second, make a commitment to change what we need to change and then follow through. Using the Serenity Prayer puts us in charge of our own happiness.

I will find as much happiness as I want today. The Serenity Prayer, used often, will be the key.

—from *A Life of My Own*

March 26

$\sim$

I plant a seed about what I want to do and then watch it take different directions.

— FRAN COYNE

Fran's openness to accepting God's involvement in his hopes and dreams makes his life far more peaceful than many of our lives may be. Trusting in a spiritual solution, the *right* turn of events for a particular situation, means having the willingness to lay our own willfulness aside. God will always have a better plan for us than we can imagine. This has always been the case, throughout our lives. It's likely that on many occasions we thwarted God's plan and caused ourselves undue pain. Have we decided to listen and to trust God's involvement now? It's never too late to try this approach.

Ruminating about the many years that have passed gives us the opportunity to see our struggles and our successes in the workplace and in the home in a new light. Those times and circumstances that caused great pain for us and others need not have been so devastating. Our resistance to the change that beckoned gave rise to our troubled state of mind. Many of us simply couldn't let go of trying to control every detail of our lives and others. God is the best manager. Do we finally understand this?

My job today is the same as every day that I have lived. I consider what I'd like to do, and then let God decide how and if it needs to be done.

— from *Keepers of the Wisdom*

March 27

What a strange pattern the shuttle of life can weave.
—FRANCES MARION

How shortsighted is our judgment about today's experiences! We'll see with clarity where they may lead us only after we've reached our destination. Of one thing we can be certain: Today's experiences, in concert with yesterday's and all that's gone before, are combining to weave an intricate life design, unique, purposeful, and for our ultimate good.

We need not feel remorse over lost chances or unproductive behavior in the past. Our destination remains the same, and our arrival is guaranteed. Our actions and decisions are never wrong. We may veer off course for a time, but the design for our lives will pull us back on the track.

The program is part of the design for our lives. It's helping us to stay on course. In fact, when we're working the Steps, we're at ease with our direction, and we trust the outcome of our efforts to the power of the program. We will add to the richness of our design, today, just as we have every day of our lives. We can anticipate today's experiences with an excited heart.

There is something special going on in my life today. I will give everybody and every event my full attention.

—from *Each Day a New Beginning*

March 28

Feeling equal to other people is a learned behavior.

We compare ourselves to others so automatically that we're seldom conscious of it. It's how we measure our worth. Feeling superior or inferior to others might be how we were raised to see the world, but there is another way. From the program we are learning that it's possible to recognize everyone's worth, to honor the equality of us all.

Practicing this new perception until it becomes automatic will have a profound impact on every circumstance in our lives. When we feel equal to others, they will no longer intimidate us and we will no longer try to shame them. Conflict will subside. Anxiety will recede. When we acknowledge them and ourselves as valuable, necessary, equal, contributing members of society, we will discover a world far different from the one we have known. And we will feel a peace, a joy, that visited us but rarely.

If I want to be at peace today, I need to remember that I am equal to everyone else.

—from *A Life of My Own*

March 29

*Things that happen aren't necessarily good or bad;
they just fit into my plans, or they don't.*

—ANNE ARTHUR

Because we are certain we know what is best for us, we seldom let our Higher Power take responsibility for the circumstances that capture our attention. More often, we map out what we think should happen, then spend hours worrying when the unexpected occurs.

It is normal for us to want our lives to unfold according to our dreams. Maturity, however, means planning for today and tomorrow and remembering not to force control over situations that involve other people. And most of our experiences include other people.

Our growth in recovery can be measured by how quickly we let God take charge of our experiences and outcomes. By turning our plans over to God and acknowledging that greater plan, we signal our readiness for the serenity this program promises.

I am guaranteed a secure partnership with a Higher Power. If I rely on that partnership today, I will feel serene, and I will instinctively know that my plan and God's are one and the same.

—from A Woman's Spirit

March 30

Each day is a new beginning.

Being here, now, is all there is. That can be a comforting idea. Whatever disrupted our lives yesterday or when we were children no longer has any control over us. Past experiences are gone forever. If we are haunted by a memory, it's our choice. But why would we want to feel sad or violated or abandoned all over again?

We hang on to the past because we think it defines all that we can be. The *Course* tells us that we are whoever we want to be. It's all in the mind. Being happy and successful and full of love for ourselves and absolutely everybody we meet seems a far-fetched dream. It can be our reality though. How? Simply experience each moment with the help and love of the Holy Spirit. Let *those* eyes see for us. Let *that* heart feel for us. Let *that* voice speak for us.

What makes us mad at any moment is really a past event triggered by the present experience. Why keep living the same old circumstances again?

I will see today as new. Nothing from my past is here, now, unless I bring it.

—from *Daily Meditations for Practicing the* Course

March 31

The future is made of the same stuff as the present.
—SIMONE WEIL

The moment is eternal. It is unending. When we move with the moment we experience all that life can offer. Being fully awake to right now guarantees rapture even when there's pain, because we know we are evolving, and we thrill with the knowledge. We are one with all that's going on around us. Our existence is purposeful and part of the whole of creation, and we can sense our purpose.

Nothing is—but now. And when we dwell on what was, or what may be, we are cut off from life—essentially dead. The only reality is the present, and it's only in the present that we are invited to make our special contribution to life; perhaps at this moment our special contribution is to reach out to another person, an act that will change two lives, ours and hers.

We must cling to the present or we'll miss its invitation to grow, to help a friend perhaps, to be part of the only reality there is. The present holds all we need and all we'll ever need to fulfill our lives. It provides every opportunity for our happiness—the only happiness there is.

Abstinence offers me the gift of the present. I will cherish it, be grateful, relish it.

—from *Each Day a New Beginning*

April

April 1

Becoming quiet brings the search for answers to an end.

Problems are opportunities for growth. They let us experience the wisdom of other people when we ask for help. They assure us a better connection to our Higher Power if we want it. And they give us chances to practice inner silence and find the place where all answers ultimately reside. Going within offers us profound calm, the love and the secure comfort of our Higher Power. Until we have sampled that gift, we can't fathom what we have missed in life. Acknowledging the presence of God changes every situation we encounter. It changes every detail of every day.

Let's not fear problems. Instead, let's see them as mere reminders that we have forgotten to remember the presence of our Higher Power. Taking a few moments to travel within will bring us clarity and comfort. Peace will come along with the problem's resolution.

I will receive the answer I need if I look in the right place.

—from *A Life of My Own*

April 2

Doing nothing is sometimes the best thing we can do.
—CONNIE HILLIARD

Recovery inspires us to change, to move forward. We set goals and count on other people to support our efforts. Having a direction is significant to us because for years many of us floundered. Now we fear regressing, so when obstacles surface, we panic. We want to take immediate action, and we want others to bend to our will. On days like this, let's remember that we still have much to learn.

It's okay to sit out a problem occasionally. Not every conflict has to be resolved or even discussed. Many circumstances need no settling. Sometimes just quieting down releases us from a problem. And in its own way, that is a decision. We are doing something. When we understand that, we'll feel better about "doing nothing." It will no longer feel like passive acceptance of a bad situation.

Often the wisest thing we can do is nothing. We have heard this advice many times at meetings and from sponsors. Let's follow it.

Before I take action on any matter today, I'll ask myself if I really need to do so. Doing nothing may be just right.

—from *A Woman's Spirit*

April 3

*I admire humor and wit. I think we develop those
qualities we admire.*

—JOANN REED

Having a well-developed sense of humor can make it possible for us to survive the most difficult of times. If we
shift our perception a bit, choosing to see the lighter side
of a situation, or if we are willing to laugh at our own
foibles, "disasters" affect us far differently. This doesn't
mean we shouldn't take life seriously, nor does it mean
there aren't real tragedies. But most tough experiences are
exaggerated in our minds. We have the capacity to perceive
them differently. Let's consider our willingness.

Medical research has recently established that laughter
is a healthy exercise, that it can actually change the outcome of an illness. Watching funny movies, as therapy, was
tried successfully by one well-known journalist who then
wrote about his experiences. He cured his disease and lived
many more years. It's not known exactly how this works
or why, but the proof is in the evidence. If laughter can
completely alleviate, or at least reduce serious conditions,
surely it can change the many tiny troubles that hinder us.
It's worth a try. Right?

As JoAnn suggests, admiring someone else's sense of
humor is the first step to improving our own. Might this
be a worthy pursuit today?

*Having a good laugh at myself or with someone else will change
how I see everything today.*

—from *Keepers of the Wisdom*

April 4

If we listen closely, we'll hear wisdom from the most unexpected sources.

We generally expect to find words of wisdom in great literature, so we look for them there. And when we listen to learned scholars, we assume their words are tempered with wisdom; thus we listen closely. At meetings we hear many words of wisdom, and oftentimes they are uttered by the newest member of the group when we least expect it.

What we are learning is that the answers we seek are always within our grasp if we open ourselves to the information that surrounds us. The program books we've been introduced to, the sponsors who offer suggestions, and the speakers at the weekly meetings all have wise words for us. Our effort to listen will reward us richly. The wise guidance we seek will come to us.

I will be alert to the utterances of everyone today. I can't assume I know who will offer the wisdom I seek.

—from *A Life of My Own*

April 5

*The wisdom of all ages and cultures emphasizes
the tremendous power our thoughts have over our
character and circumstances.*

—LIANE CORDES

"As we think, so we are." We are gifted with the personal power to make thoughtful choices and thus decide who we are. Our actions and choices combine to create our character, and our character influences the circumstances of our lives.

Our personal mind power will work to our advantage when we think positively, or it will contribute to our disadvantage. Imagining our good fortunes will prepare us for them. Imagining the successful completion of a task heightens and strengthens the commitment we must make daily to it. Imagining the steps necessary to the successful accomplishment of any goal directs our efforts so we don't falter along the way. Our minds work powerfully for our good. And just as powerfully to our detriment, when fears intrude on all our thoughts.

The program has given me positive personal power; it lies in the relationship I have with my higher power. My outlook and attitude toward life reveal the strength of my connection to God. I will work with God and imagine my good fortune today.

—from *Each Day a New Beginning*

April 6

You need few basic things for a vital age: purposes and projects, and bonds of intimacy.

—BETTY FRIEDAN

Feeling needed is what it all adds up to. We didn't doubt our value when we were raising our families and bringing home a paycheck. We knew we were needed when a child or parent or spouse came to us for advice. Friends sharing their innermost secrets with us made us feel special, too. But now, none of these things may be prevalent in our lives. It's not unusual for people our age to feel worthless. The responsibility for changing that feeling rests with us.

If being involved, whether on the job or with friends, gave our lives meaning when we were young, we at least have an understanding of how to regain that sense of well-being now. We certainly don't need a job to do it, but we do need to make an offering of some kind to the world at large. And we must have a friend, a confidant, we share ourselves with fully. Knowing that we make a difference in someone's life, anyone's life, gets us out of bed and on the bus every morning.

It's not all that hard to find a project or a friend. We simply have to want to.

I will enrich my life by sharing it with someone else today. I don't even have to know who this person will be until I "get there."

—from Keepers of the Wisdom

April 7

Nothing is ever missing from our lives but our awareness of God.

When the house payment is overdue and our children are truant from school and the job we so desperately wanted went to someone else, it's not easy to believe that all we need is to remember God. The other problems seem so real. And in one respect they are. We do have to acknowledge them and decide on a plan of action. But we don't have to keep our focus on "poor me." Instead, we can recall that the Holy Spirit, God's gift to us, will comfort us and give us guidance.

Whatever is happening around us doesn't have to determine how we feel. We can feel consistently happy and secure, even in the most troubling of times, if we remember we are partners with God, that the Holy Spirit is always present, and that all our experiences serve to teach us. We need not be scared or angry, ever. All is well.

Knowing that God never went away reminds us that when we feel alone, it is only we who have turned away. The solution is simply to turn back.

Today I will say to God, "Here I am. Tell me what to do." I'll not be ignored.

—from *Daily Meditations for Practicing the* Course

April 8

If what we are doing with our anger is not achieving the desired result, it would seem logical to try something different.

—HARRIET LERNER

How productive is anger? There is more than one school of thought. Some say we addicts can't afford to be angry. Others warn against repressing it. Learning simply to recognize anger is a big step for many of us. One thing we all agree on is that anger is a powerful feeling that affects us in many ways. If it goes unacknowledged, our relations with others are damaged.

Anger is uncomfortable for many of us. We feel it often enough, but it makes us nervous anyway. Frequently we think we must be doing something wrong or we wouldn't be angry. Sometimes that's true. However, anger always signals that it's time to assess what we are projecting onto the situations or the people in our midst. Anger doesn't just happen. It's sown and cultivated by us.

If I get angry today I will look for the reason within myself. I can't change others, but I can change myself.

—from *A Woman's Spirit*

April 9

*It is never the circumstances, but only our thoughts
about circumstances, that create our state of mind.*
—JANE NELSEN

We all have at least one friend who seems unruffled by the
unpredictable and changing circumstances of her life. How
does she do it? People like her seem to trust that God is in
charge and all things are happening for our ultimate good.
While we scurry around, fretting and controlling as much
as we can—usually to no avail—she stays quiet and feels
blessed by her life.

The difference between her and us is the frantic activity
that consumes our minds. We tend to react continuously
to the events around us. Until now, observing events rather
than reacting to them was never an option. But taking
charge of our lives in this fashion releases our anxiety and
fills us with peace. With time and practice we'll experience
the serenity that our friend feels.

*I have control of my thoughts. Nothing can upset me today unless I
choose to let it.*

—from *A Woman's Spirit*

April 10

Sometimes it's worse to win a fight than to lose.
—BILLIE HOLIDAY

Our struggles with other people always take their toll on us. They often push us to behavior we're not proud of. They may result in irreparable rifts. They frequently trigger an emotional relapse. No battle is worth the damage to the psyche that nearly any battle can cause. Nonresistance is the safer way to chart our daily course.

Bowing with the wind, flowing with the tide, eases the steps we need to take, the steps that will carry us to our personal fulfillment. Part of the process of our growth is learning to slide past the negative situations that confront us, coming to understand that we are in this life to fulfill a unique purpose. The many barriers that get in our way can strengthen our reliance on God if we'll let them. We need never be thwarted by people or situations. We will profit from taking all experiences in our stride. The course we travel is the one we chart. The progress we make toward our life goals is proportionate to the smoothness of our steps.

I will flow with the tide. It will assuredly move me closer to my destination.

—from *Each Day a New Beginning*

April 11

To let go means to stop.

The disease of alcoholism has affected us too. One of the signs is wanting every circumstance that touches us to be handled our way, right now! What often happens is that we take over the responsibilities of someone else. Conflict arises, a power struggle ensues, and a relationship is once again strained.

There are moments when we can't imagine letting go of an outcome, at least not when we will be affected. It's fortunate that other people testify to how well their lives are going since they have dared to let go, because that gives us courage to do the same. When we finally do let go, we realize first how free we feel. Second, we are peaceful. Third, the tension, so common to our relationships, is gone.

To let go means to stop: stop talking, stop arguing, stop manipulating, stop whining, stop fantasizing about what should be, stop every action that is meant to control or change someone else. The result will be transformed lives, ours and those close to us.

I will stop whatever I'm about to do today and think it through. If I'm intent on changing someone else, I'll stop myself.

—from *A Life of My Own*

April 12

Everybody has what it takes to express himself.
—JANICE CLARK

Talent has been bestowed on all of us. We doubt this only because, regardless of age, we compare ourselves with others too often. We fail to see that our callings are unique, not quite like anyone else's, and that we aren't really comparable to them. We've been told this for years. Why do we disbelieve it anyway?

There is no time like the present for changing our philosophy about life. But how do we begin? Let's start by accepting the fact that we are blessed with gifts that are unique to us. Next, let's assume that the people who come into our lives—who have been coming into our lives for decades—are in need of what we, and only we, can give. Additionally, let's continually extend compliments to others for their achievements, quietly being thankful for our own as well.

We can learn to believe in our strengths, seeing them as our special talents, by earnestly deciding that they are so. It's a simple, but profound, change in attitude. We can do it.

My talent can be expressed in many ways today. The easiest is to lovingly acknowledge the presence of others. The rest will follow.

—from *Keepers of the Wisdom*

April 13

Be still and listen to the stillness within.
—DARLENE LARSON JENKS

No answer eludes us if we turn to the source of all answers—
the stillness within. Prayer accompanied by meditation will
always provide the answers we need for the situations fac-
ing us. The answers we want are not guaranteed, however.
We must trust that we will be directed to take the right
steps. Our well-being is assured if we let go of being the
one in control and turn our wills over to the care of God,
our messenger within.

How comforting to know that all answers are as close
as our quiet moments. God never chooses to keep the answers from us. We simply fail to quiet our thoughts long
enough to heed them. Our minds race, obsessively, all too
often. We jump from one scenario to another, one fear to
another, one emotion to another. And each time our
thoughts capture a new focus, we push the answer we seek
further into the background.

*The process is simple, if I want to follow it. The answers await me
if I truly want them. I need only sit quietly and ask God to offer
the guidance I need. And then I will sit quietly some more.*

—from *Each Day a New Beginning*

April 14

A healed mind cannot attack.

We are journeying toward healed minds. That's our purpose in this life. Unfortunately, we don't always remember what a healed mind is. That's because maintaining a constant connection to the love of God is elusive and many of us have only brief successes.

Remembering that any person's outburst of anger is a call for healing and help lessens our need to strike back. Of course, the urge to do so may be there, sometimes powerfully so. But with practice we can strengthen our reliance on the Holy Spirit to guide our responses to every person we encounter. We will never want to attack even the most disruptive individuals if we remember the pain that underlies their behavior.

My mind can practice being healed today. I can look with a loving heart on everyone I meet.

—from *Daily Meditations for Practicing the* Course

April 15

One of the attributes of love . . . is to bring harmony
and order out of chaos.

—MOLLY HASKELL

Have we forgotten how to live in our hurried passage
through life? Perhaps we need reminding that love focuses
our attention and guides our direction. Our actions aren't
hurried and our feelings aren't confused and unraveled
when we're loving others and ourselves. Love offers form
and enhancement to each moment.

When we experience the love of another, we remember
our importance, and theirs, to the circle of life, and we feel
encouraged, at times even impelled, to share the enchant-
ment of love with someone new.

When the day's frantic activities crowd the heart's silent
places, we must slow our pace and take notice of the loved
ones in our presence, there by intent, remembering with
them the design that has captured us and given meaning
to our lives.

Love creates music from the disharmony of our hap-
hazard life choices. Giving it away is like a song of happiness emerging from our hearts.

—from *Worthy of Love*

April 16

❧

Retreat is not defeat!
—KAY LOVATT

Sometimes the most productive thing we can do is back away from a situation that's causing us pain. Every time we feel compelled to resolve a crisis, we can retreat, at least for a time. Giving our emotions a rest gives us a fresh perspective.

Trying to force another person to see a situation as we do seldom works, just as we can't be convinced against our will that someone else is right. The history we carry colors our view. But we can learn from one another; that's why we are sharing this journey.

Does it seem that we encourage conflicts? Is our security tied to having others validate our opinions? Perhaps turning to our Higher Power each time we anticipate conflict will relieve us of the need to express an opinion that's not crucial to the moment.

I don't have to resolve anything today. I can simply go along with how things are and trust that they will change, with God's help.

—from A Woman's Spirit

April 17

*Never turn down a job because you think it's too
small; you don't know where it can lead.*
—JULIA MORGAN

How short is our vision of where an invitation might take
us! Any invitation. Of one thing we can be certain, it offers
an opportunity for making a choice, which means taking
responsibility for who we're becoming. Choice-making is
growth-enhancing because it strengthens our awareness
of personal power.

Our lives unfold in small measures, just as small as they
need to be for our personal comfort. It's doubtful that we
could handle everything the future has in store, today;
however, we will be prepared for it, measure by measure,
choice by choice, day by day. We need not fear; what is
meted out to us in the invitations offered is for our benefit. We are on a pathway to goodness.

The thrill of making choices is new to many of us when
we enter this program. We'd opted for the passive life, all
too often, and we became increasingly aware of, and often
depressed by, our self-imposed powerlessness. Free at last!
We are free at last to fully participate in our lives.

*I will be grateful for the many options to act tugging at me today.
Every choice I make strengthens my womanhood.*

—from Each Day a New Beginning

April 18

As we cultivate stillness and commune with the Presence within, we are mightily enhanced.

—MARSHA SINETAR

When we retreat to our quiet interior spaces, we grow in our understanding of God and life's mysteries. The richness we come to know through keeping our spiritual life simple is unexpected.

Spiritual leaders from all faiths have suggested we go within to know God and, thus, ourselves. The founders of our program suggested likewise. It was their hope that we might find the peace and freedom that only God can guarantee. The Steps are our tools for knowing God.

Each day that we rely on our spiritual connection to clarify our direction, we'll discover the serenity that enhances our being. Perhaps we didn't need our dependencies to know God, but they are serving as the pathway to our freedom.

I consider myself lucky to be an alcoholic or other drug addict. It has given me a connection to God that is enriching my life.

—from *A Woman's Spirit*

April 19

Alcoholics suffer from "self-will run riot." We do too!

Being certain that we were right, that our way was the right way, was part of our old lives. Many of us fell into the habit of picking up the pieces when a spouse or other family member made a mess of some situation. And that fueled our belief that we knew best.

In regard to some circumstances, we probably do know best. After all, each of us is right some of the time. But learning to back off from a situation, even when it appears we are right, empowers us. Not *having* to be right gives us a new freedom. It lessens the tension between us and other people. It relieves us of the burden of trying to make outcomes match our expectations.

Our path through life will be easier to navigate if we try to be right only regarding ourselves.

Today I will only decide what's right for me.

—from *A Life of My Own*

April 20

Attitude is everything!

Today will be what we make it. Regardless of the weather, the kinds of work to be done, the personalities crossing our paths, we'll feel joy and peace if that is our choice.

Agonizing over circumstances that aren't to our liking or dwelling on our failure to control other people, whether friends or foes, has robbed us of the happiness that is always ours to experience. Depression, anger, fear, and frustration shadowed our steps because we didn't take control of the only thing that's ever been in our control absolutely—attitude.

It's so easy to blame others for every wrinkle in our lives. But as we grow accustomed to the idea of taking full responsibility for how we think and feel, we'll be empowered. No longer will our sense of self feel diminished. And, as Abraham Lincoln is credited with saying, we will be just as happy as we make up our minds to be.

Nobody can mess with my attitude but me!

—from *A Life of My Own*

April 21

~O

My spiritual life has changed in the last few years.
—JAMES CASEY

Most of us have expanded our understanding of "the spiritual life." We may have grown up in religious homes. At our age, that wouldn't be unusual. But now we realize that didn't necessarily mean we were encouraged to be spiritual. The idea of "spirituality" might have been suspect, even. To our parents it may have sounded like the occult rather than a church affiliation.

What spirituality meant to Jim, and perhaps means to many of us, is having a relationship we nurture with the Creator, however we define that. It means believing we have an inner voice that is eager to offer us guidance whenever we are at a loss about what to do. Practicing a spiritual life also relieves us of the burden of worry about the future. We know it will take care of itself, in the same way as we'll be taken care of.

As we move through life, we continue to be confronted by conflict and problems over which we have no control. That's the learning curve, nothing more. We'll always be on this path. The good news is that our response to the struggle will change in proportion to our willingness to seek God's help.

How I see God and my life should keep changing. Will I do my part to open my eyes wider today?

—from *Keepers of the Wisdom*

April 22

Attack or love, that's all there is.

Attack wears many disguises. Sometimes it looks like a thoughtful suggestion, sometimes an educated opinion. Occasionally we choose to explain our attacks as being assertive. The silent treatment is another common way to attack. There are many forms, and some are quite creative. The result is always the same, however. We may win the battle, but we lose the war.

Choosing love, the alternative response, isn't so hard once we make up our minds to try it. It becomes even easier to choose it again once we've made the initial selection. And it is much less stressful. It doesn't take an elaborate plan to approach the other person or circumstance. We simply put our heart first and the rest follows.

I have an easy day ahead if I give only love.

—from *Daily Meditations for Practicing the* Course

April 23

We are told all we need to know.

We often crave to know every detail of every moment of the rest of our lives, but we don't need them. We couldn't handle them, really. We are given all the information we need as the moments tick by. The Holy Spirit knows far better than what we need to know, and when. And we'll always find it out when the time is right.

When we grow in our acceptance of this principle, our lives will grow simpler. Our task is to turn to the Holy Spirit, not the ego, for direction. Our minds contain them both, of course. Recognizing their separate voices comes with practice and the willingness to be peaceful rather than "right."

Our lives don't become less exciting when we let the Holy Spirit be in charge. In fact, some might say that going along for the ride, rather than steering the car, offers us unexpected adventure and surprise.

Letting someone else decide the route leaves me free to enjoy the many stops on the way.

—from *Daily Meditations for Practicing the* Course

April 24

Listening is a wonderful gift we can choose to open each day.

Intently listening to each person who crosses our path is a most difficult assignment. But only by listening do we gather our daily lessons and significant messages from our Higher Power. When it's hard to listen because we don't like what someone is saying, we have to consider why. Evaluating our own perceptions and letting go of others' opinions are important lessons.

We all play key roles in each others' lives. It's not coincidental that we share this path at this time. The people we meet, work with, live with—all are necessary to our Divine journey. From this program we are gathering the tools that will ease the steps of our journey. Listening is a significant tool. Let's be glad for every opportunity to strengthen our listening skills.

My mind may wander when I talk with a friend today, but with God's help, I'll remember that I need to hear what is said.

—from *A Life of My Own*

April 25

When people bother you in any way, it is because their souls are trying to get your divine attention and your blessing.

—CATHERINE PONDER

We are in constant communication with one another and, in the spiritual realm, with God. No matter how singular our particular course may appear, our path is running parallel to many paths. And all paths will intersect when the need is present. The point of intersection is the moment when another soul seeks our attention. We can be attentive and loving to the people seeking our attention. Their growth and ours is at stake.

We can be grateful for our involvement with other lives. We can be mindful that our particular blessing is like no one else's and that we all need input from the many significant persons in our lives. There is no insignificant encounter in our passage through life. Each juncture with someone else is part of the destiny of both participants.

I will look carefully and lovingly at the people around me today and bless them, one and all. They are in my life because they need to be. I, likewise, need them.

—from *Each Day a New Beginning*

April 26

Life is perfect, just the way it is and just the way it
is not.

—PEGGY BASSETT

Coming to believe that life is perfect however it is takes
willingness and concentrated faith. Most of us waste precious hours every day wishing for something that isn't.
Will we ever learn?

It isn't wrong to want some things to be different. If
our own behavior can inspire positive changes in ourselves
or others, then it's not wrong to take responsibility for
what we can do. What is futile, though, is assuming we
know what is best for everyone. We can't see the big picture. God gives us only what we need right now. What may
look like trouble, what may appear as imperfect one
minute, may be God's greater plan. Let's wait and see.

*I will find comfort in the message that all is well. I will use that
today if I get worried about how events seem to be unfolding.*

—from *A Woman's Spirit*

April 27

Our experiences depend on our outlook.

Doesn't everybody get mad at unruly children? Surely a downpour in the midst of an outing is depressing. And a job loss can't be anything but discouraging. Or can it? It's quite a revelation to note how differently each of us responds to our experiences. Seeing a glass as half-full rather than half-empty is clearly our decision.

Many of us have suffered from negative attitudes. Until we discovered a Twelve Step program, we didn't understand that it was within our power to relish all our experiences, to see them as points on our learning curve, to recognize that every experience is meant to bless our journey.

Life passes so quickly, and we have so much to learn along the way. Accepting every moment as sacred and just what we need relieves us of the tendency to judge experiences negatively.

Whatever comes to me today can be relished. I am "in process."

—from *A Life of My Own*

April 28

...

... words are more powerful than perhaps anyone suspects, and once deeply engraved in a child's mind, they are not easily eradicated.

—MAY SARTON

How burdened we became, as little girls, with the labels applied by parents, teachers, even school chums. We believe about ourselves what others teach us to believe. The messages aren't always overt. But even the very subtle ones are etched in our minds, and they remind us of our "shortcomings" long into adulthood.

Try as we might to forget the criticisms, the names, they linger in our memories and influence our self-perceptions as adults. The intervening years have done little to erase whatever emotional scars we acquired as children.

Our partnership with God will help us understand that we are spiritual beings with a wonderful purpose in this life. And we are as lovely, as capable, as successful as we perceive ourselves to be. Our own thoughts and words, our own labels can become as powerful as those of our youth. It takes practice to believe in ourselves. But we can break the past's hold on us.

My higher power will help me know the real me. I am all that I ever needed to be; I am special, and I will come to believe that.

—from *Each Day a New Beginning*

April 29

Advice from others applies to them.
—GEORGETTE VICKSTROM

Those of us who share this program are learning how to care about others, and it is natural that we want to help one another. Of course, that means we may suggest, sometimes too strongly, what we think a friend ought to do. We are frequently on the receiving end of similar suggestions. We can be glad that others want to help. We suffered alone with our problems for far too long. However, no one's advice can exactly fit our situation. Nor can ours fit theirs. The perspective that guides each of us is unique to our experiences.

It is never wrong to offer our support. Nor is it wrong, if asked, to share what we would do if the problem were ours. But to say to anyone, "Here is what you should do," is harmful. Let God play God.

I will not give unwanted suggestions or advice to anyone today. God is the best guide for each of us.

—from *A Woman's Spirit*

April 30

A miracle is merely a shift, a change, in perception.

How hard can it be to "change our minds"? Our personal histories would suggest that we have changed our minds many times. We've moved, changed jobs, changed marriages and relationships, left friends behind. But the *Course* says we're ready for a new understanding of what "change" means.

Life changes were generally the result of an active ego. Some of the changes may have been positive. However, if the ego inspired them, they weren't miracles. They were still attempts to control our lives or the lives of others. Real miracles come from changing our minds, not other people or situations. We are learning the difference now.

The shift in perception we are learning about engages only our hearts, never the ego. We need merely to ask for the shift and it will come; our request is granted. The Holy Spirit wants us to be peaceful, to have the miracle. Let us ask for it.

I can have one or more miracles today.

—from *Daily Meditations for Practicing the* Course

May

May 1

*I have thought on many things
And after thinking find
One's world is not a stable thing
But a product of the mind.*

—IDA BELLEGARDE

Understanding and accepting Ida's philosophy simplifies our lives. It guarantees that what we dwell on, we'll experience. Another way of saying it is, "As we think, so we are." This puts us in the driver's seat, so to speak, but not all of us want the responsibility for how our lives are unfolding. We have had and we will have whatever experiences we desire in this life. That's a thrilling, awesome, sometimes fearful thought.

Often we have marveled at how easily some others go through life. They seem to avoid the calamities that befall us. Considering Ida's simple poem for a moment gives us another perspective. Those who sail through life have quite probably *pictured* a different set of experiences for themselves. They are not favored by the gods; they simply use their minds to a sweeter advantage. Rest assured, we can do the same.

Today is mine to picture and enjoy. A moment's contemplation will give me what I long for.

—from *Keepers of the Wisdom*

May 2

❧

Loving others begins with respect.

So many books have been written on "how to love" that many of us assume we don't know how and maybe will never learn. We can simplify the process, however, by focusing on the Golden Rule. For starters, we can treat others as respectfully as we'd like to be treated. People respond well to respect, and they often pay us respect in return.

Next, let's put the needs of at least one other person ahead of our own today. It's imperative that we do it willingly, not resentfully. We can ask God to help us. We'll discover an unexpected benefit: Not being self-absorbed for a change is really quite refreshing.

Finally, we can ask God for freedom from the thinking that keeps us from loving others. Each person who enters our circle of experience today can be loved by us if we are willing to turn to God for help.

Loving others is easier if I keep it simple. I will focus on courtesy today.

—from *A Life of My Own*

May 3

Problems have only the size and the power that you give them.

—S. H.

We will not be free from all difficulties today, or during any period of our lives. But we have the personal power to eliminate the threat, the sting of any challenge. But it's our vision of circumstances that gives them their interpretation.

At this moment, we are defining our experience. We are labeling events good or bad, valuable or meaningless. And our growth, particularly this day, is greatly influenced by the value judgments we attach to our experiences.

As we grow stronger emotionally and spiritually, we learn that all difficulties are truly opportunities for exceptional growth and increased awareness of the truth of existence. All experiences can be taken in stride if we are trustful of their intended blessing.

We are sharing this life, every moment of it, with a power greater than ourselves. We need not worry about any circumstance. Always we are watched over. We never need struggle alone.

We can let go of our problems. It's ourselves and the attitude we have cultivated that make any situation a problem. We can turn it loose and therein discover the solution.

I will not make mountains out of the molehills in my life.

—from *Each Day a New Beginning*

May 4

*I have discovered that while God would do for me
what I could not do for myself, God would not do
for me what I could do for myself.*

—MARY NORTON GORDON

There are some things God is always in charge of. One is
outcomes. Another is the big picture encompassing our
lives. Each experience is part of God's design for us. On occasion, we may feel there is little for us to do, since God
will handle it all. However, the truth is, our participation
is necessary. Every day we have many opportunities to
thoughtfully put one foot in front of the other. How lovingly, how gently, how honestly and openly we move
through our lives—all these things color the experiences
God has planned for us.

We may sometimes find ourselves sitting back, waiting
for God to take charge, or aggressively trying to force an
outcome that belongs only to God. But we are learning.
With time in the program, we begin to realize what is
God's work and what is ours. Our sponsors, the women
who share their experiences in meetings, prayer, and meditation, enlighten us about how it works.

*I am surrounded by women who can help me distinguish between
my job and God's job today. My confusion won't trouble me for
long.*

—from *A Woman's Spirit*

May 5

Forgiveness is the path to peacefulness.

Coming to believe that all disharmony may be the result of even a single, still-harbored resentment gives us a refreshing new look at our lives. We are only as upset as our willingness to let old memories control us. We can be free of them—now! It's a decision to let the past go. It's a decision to ask the Holy Spirit for a new perspective. It's a decision to ask, again and again, if we fall into the old, more familiar pattern of disharmony.

Who among us would admit to preferring agitation to peacefulness? Few at best. However, many of us live as though that's the case. We get mad and stay mad. We argue and then relive the tension for hours or days. New experiences with unsuspecting companions carry the stamp of earlier encounters that left us furious. We can change all of this. It's not so very difficult, in fact.

The Holy Spirit is always with us. Of course, so is the ego. Which one we honor will determine our level of peacefulness.

I will be as peaceful as I decide today. Getting free of resentment through forgiveness is the key.

—from *Daily Meditations for Practicing the* Course

May 6

Fear triggers attack.

Any attack, whether verbal or physical, is caused by fear. When contemplating an attack, we need to ask ourselves, "What is causing the fear?" That's the issue to consider, and the answer is always the same. Fear occurs when we align ourselves with the ego. Fear has no life of its own.

The urge to attack another person is manageable. We can always curtail the impulse if we are willing to seek the help of the Holy Spirit. Its voice is softer than the voice of the ego, so we have to grow quiet to hear it. But we'll see our "opponent" quite differently after listening to the Spirit.

The Holy Spirit is capable only of love. If we are not at peace in a situation, or if we harbor any thought other than love, we are not aligned with the quiet voice. The only barrier to feeling love is the one the ego constructs. We are lucky that its voice can be ignored in an instant.

The voice I hear today determines my level of peace.

—from *Daily Meditations for Practicing the* Course

May 7

When love beckons to you, follow him, though his ways are hard and steep.

—KAHLIL GIBRAN

There will be many opportunities to express love in the days ahead, and some may be cloaked in harsh wrappings. Perhaps an argument will wound and then be healed by the exchange of loving words and intimate gestures.

Maybe a friend or lover will be called away for a while, and the painful loneliness will make us question our commitment to love. Yet, in loving unconditionally, we'll find peace.

Love, though a soft word and a gentle image, doesn't always promise us soft, gentle moments. Sometimes love offers us a pained heart and empty arms. We know love comforts, but not always. Love heals, but in its own time. The desire to know love draws us together, always.

—from *Worthy of Love*

May 8

*I cannot have what I want if I do not wish it
for others.*

Envy is familiar to many of us. We may spend far too much
time comparing ourselves with others and grading ourselves as inadequate. Focusing on what others have never
allows us to feel grateful for our blessings or generous in
spirit. Paradoxically, what we want for *others* comes back
to *us*.

This is a simple principle, but like other new ideas, we
have to "wear it" for a while to get its meaning; we have to
practice it faithfully to get its effect. Perhaps initially we
can better see its reverse. Let's recall a few times when we
have harbored mean thoughts toward another or wished
ill will on an acquaintance. Our own spirit felt the reper-
cussions. Maybe bad luck didn't overtly trip us, but we
never feel good for long when we cultivate a mean-spirited
attitude. Everyone is served by our good wishes. Let's work
on that today.

*If I catch myself feeling jealous or mean, I'll take charge of my
thoughts. Only I can turn them around.*

—from *A Woman's Spirit*

May 9

Beginnings are apt to be shadowy.
—RACHEL CARSON

When we embark on a new career, open an unfamiliar door, begin a loving relationship, we can seldom see nor can we even anticipate where the experience may take us. At our best we can see only what this day brings. We can trust with certainty that we will be safely led through the "shadows."

To make gains in this life we must venture forth to new places, contact new people, chance new experiences. Even though we may be fearful of the new, we must go forward. It's comforting to remember that we never take any step alone. It is our destiny to experience many new beginnings. And a dimension of the growth process is to develop trust that each of these experiences will in time comfort us and offer us the knowledge our inner self awaits. Without the new beginnings we are unable to fulfill the purpose for which we've been created.

No new beginning is more than we can handle. Every new beginning is needed by our developing selves, and we are ready for whatever comes.

I will look to my new beginnings gladly. They are special to the growth I am now ready for.

—from *Each Day a New Beginning*

May 10

Conflicts can be avoided.

We get into conflicts with other people because of us, not them. We can walk away from circumstances that are beginning to boil. We can decide that feeling peaceful is more important than forcing an opinion on someone else. And we can choose to seek God's guidance in every tense situation. Making these choices gets easier with practice, but at first we can't imagine not having the last word.

Many of us have too much invested in being right. Perhaps we think our worth relies on others' agreeing with our opinions. If we use the *right* words, a really good argument, we can sway their opinion, we hope. Sometimes we're successful. Unfortunately, that fuels our fire to push our opinion the next time too.

Deciding to accept that all people have a right to their opinion is a big change for us. Coming to believe that each of us is on a unique journey helps us make that decision.

The program is helping me understand other people. Today I'll walk away from every opportunity to argue with someone. The other person's perspective is as valid as my own.

—from *A Life of My Own*

May 11

*If you argue with a person who is unbalanced,
after a few minutes it's hard to tell which one of
you is unbalanced.*

—JIM BURNS

Differing opinions and perspectives add a richness to life. There would be no incentive to broaden our understanding of anything, to change how we perceive people or circumstances, if we found ourselves in agreement with everyone every moment. So being in absolute agreement isn't the goal; however, being willing to accept others' opinions freely, without the need to change them, is. The curious thing, of course, is that when others don't try to change us or our opinions, but honor whatever view we have, we feel more willing to open our minds to something new. And vice versa.

The lucky among us learned long ago that it was no reflection on us when others didn't agree with our opinions. Some of us are still struggling to believe that. A good way to check out this idea, though, is to take note of how certain admired friends respond to adversity or a very opinionated person. We always marvel at how they can smile and walk away from a conflict. They have no special talent. They have merely learned, earlier than ourselves, the more important quality of respect and acceptance. "Being right" is always a matter of degree and perspective. Being at peace is always a matter of choice.

I can choose peace rather than trying to "sell" an opinion today.

—from *Keepers of the Wisdom*

May 12

To listen is to hear with one's heart.

Keeping silent while a friend is talking should not be confused with listening. Dialog can fill our minds even when friends are sharing the most intimate details of their lives. Why is it so difficult to listen?

Our listening impairment probably began in childhood. We feared we didn't measure up, so we were constantly obsessed with what other people thought of us. Worry became a way of life, and we seldom distinguished between the trivial and the important. We learned to keep our minds trapped in thought.

Listening with our heart is a new skill. When we try it, we'll first be touched by the emotion contained in the message being shared. Then our own worry thoughts will recede. Letting another's pain or joy reach our hearts will enrich us. We will come to understand that paying loving attention to someone's story will offer us answers we didn't even know we needed.

It's not coincidental if a friend comes to me in need today. I'll receive the guidance I need through what is shared.

—from *A Life of My Own*

May 13

*On any journey, we must find out where we are
before we can plan the first step.*

—KATHY BOEVINK

Our lives in all aspects are a journey toward a destination,
one fitting to our purpose, our special gifts, our particular
needs as women. Each day contributes to our journey, carrying us closer to our destination. However, we often take
a circuitous route. We get stranded or waylaid by our selfish desires, by the intrusion of our controlling ego.

We can reflect on the progress we've made toward our
destination, the steps we've taken that have unknowingly
contributed to our journey. Our easiest steps have been
the ones we took in partnership with God. It's in God's
mind that our path is well marked.

We are just where we need to be today. The experiences
that we meet are like points on the map of our journey.
Some of them are rest stops. Others resemble high-speed
straightaways. The journey to our destination is not always smooth, but the more we let God sit in the driver's
seat, the easier will be our ride.

*I will plan my journey today with God's help, and my ride will be
smooth.*

—from Each Day a New Beginning

May 14

We are all diamonds in the rough.
—ROSEANN LLOYD

We tend to exaggerate our own imperfections and glorify other women's strengths. In reality, we are all imperfect yet quite good enough. Since getting clean and sober and joining this sisterhood of recovery, we have been given the tools for smoothing the rough edges of our character. Becoming a real gem is within our reach.

How do we begin? It's important to keep our efforts simple. Because we have so much we want to change, many of us try to change everything about ourselves overnight. The result is overwhelming frustration. We became who we are now over many years of reckless living. We must be realistic. Committing to one tiny change a day is enough to focus on. And it's more than enough to eventually bring about the overall changes we seek.

When we accept that who we are right now is okay with God, we'll also accept the pace of our progress in becoming who we want to be.

Watching my facets begin to sparkle can make each day a thrill to live. I'll appreciate the opportunities to polish my rough edges today.

—from *A Woman's Spirit*

May 15

Be still and know.

What does it mean to be still? What are we trying to know? These are serious questions. Having minds that run non-stop seems the norm. It's who we are, after all. Experiencing the quiet within feels like doing nothing. And we've been programmed to think we need to be doing something all the time. To stand still is to get left behind, we think.

Let's pretend for a spell that it's okay to be idle. Let's take this as an opportunity for a new way of living. With every thought that comes, let it float away. With every desire to speak, let the moment pass. Every moment can be forfeited. Feel the freedom of doing nothing, saying nothing, thinking nothing, for even a few moments. Peace does come. Peace at last.

We can't be sure we'll know anything specific in this quiet, but we will know what we need to. Within the quiet lie all answers.

I will give up my mad thinking for a few moments today.

—from *Daily Meditations for Practicing the* Course

May 16

To forgive is to join with others.

No doubt at least one circumstance will arise today that can trigger anger. Even minor disturbances push our buttons if we're not vigilant. The question many of us have is, "What's wrong with anger?" We've heard that it's healthy to admit anger, that we shouldn't stuff it. Have we been misguided?

From the *Course* we learn that anger is about us, not the others on our path. Therefore, expressing it by attacking someone else doesn't properly address the cause. If we're the sole source of what is irritating us, we're also the single source of forgiveness, and thus change and healing. Actually, this simplifies our lives. It just isn't possible to make others behave, but it is possible to change how we act, feel, and think. The unexpected miracle is that everything and everyone else will be changed in the process.

I am as happy as I choose to be today. My anger is gone when I acknowledge its source and its solution.

—from *Daily Meditations for Practicing the* Course

May 17

We can find value in most experiences.

We can never know, absolutely, what God's plan for our lives is. Yet we can trust that there is one and that we are being watched over. Almost every day an experience troubles us. Maybe it's a phone call from a drunk friend or criticism from a boss. So quickly we judge its meaning for our lives. But from the experiences we were certain we couldn't live through we garnered important knowledge and growth. Today's experiences too will be understood in time.

Because we don't know just where God is taking us, we can't possibly anticipate all that we'll need to know. That's where God's plan comes in. We will be given our lessons when the time is right. We won't be led into situations we're unprepared for. And we'll have to trust that each circumstance we do face is necessary and part of our unfolding.

When we wonder, why me? let's remember how lucky we are to still be fulfilling God's plan.

My recovery is as much a part of God's plan as was my obsessive codependency. I'm in a position to help other people now. Today's interactions will lend purpose to my life.

—from *A Life of My Own*

May 18

~⚬

Pain is inevitable. Suffering is optional.
—KATHLEEN CASEY

How awesome is our power, personally, to choose our attitudes and our responses to any situation, to every situation. We will feel only how we choose to feel, no matter the circumstance. Happiness is as free an option as sorrow.

Perceiving our challenges as opportunities for positive growth rather than stumbling blocks in our path to success is a choice readily available. What is inevitable—a matter over which we have no choice—is that difficult times, painful experiences will visit us. We can, however, greet them like welcome guests, celebrating their blessings on us and the personal growth they inspire.

No circumstance demands suffering. Every circumstance has a silver lining. In one instance you may choose to feel self-pity; in the next, gladness.

We do not always feel confident about our choices, even when we accept the responsibility for making them. How lucky for us that the program offers a solution! Prayer and meditation, guidance from our higher power, can help us make the right choice every time.

I will relish my freedom to choose, to feel, to act. I and only I can take it away.

—from *Each Day a New Beginning*

May 19

*Strangely, it was comforting to me when I read
that squirrels forget where they hide about half
their nuts.*

—RUTH CASEY

We sometimes set unreasonably high standards for ourselves. Instead of being content with average, we think we must be perfect or we don't count. The problem is that none of us can be perfect in every endeavor. To be human is to be fallible. And that's okay, even though we don't often believe it.

God doesn't expect perfection. How often have we been reminded of that since joining this program? What God does expect is that we do our best and do it lovingly. Whether we are at work, at home cooking dinner for the family, or at the bedside of an ailing friend or lover, we need only give the task our focused attention and willing heart. The joy we feel as the result of our efforts will convince us that we have been as close to perfect as we need to be.

I will do the best I can today if I am determined to be attentive to the task at hand and loving in my attitude.

—from A Woman's Spirit

May 20

Our words, unless loving, need not be spoken.

It's only human to think we're always right and to assume others need enlightenment. Many unnecessary arguments follow. The more familiar we become with the principles of this program, the easier it will be to respect that others have opinions too. Sharing our view is one thing; trying to force it on someone else is quite another!

Since joining this fellowship, we have been exposed to so many new tools, one of which is keeping our thoughts and opinions, unless loving, to ourselves. This tool wields significant impact. It changes how we are perceived. Even more importantly, it changes how we perceive others. To look through eyes that are loving, and to speak words that reflect *that* view, changes every moment of our lives every day.

I can be a person even I'd look up to today. It's all a matter of how I speak and what I say.

—from *A Life of My Own*

May 21

*Do not compare yourself with others, for you are
a unique and wonderful creation. Make your own
beautiful footprints in the snow.*

—BARBARA KIMBALL

Comparisons we make of ourselves to other women do destruction far greater than our conscious minds are aware of. Positioning ourselves or her on the "beloved pedestal" prevents the equality of sisterhood that offers each woman the freedom to be solely herself.

Comparisons in which we are the losers darken the moment, cut us off from the actual rhythms of that moment. The consequences can be grave. Within any moment might be the opportunity we've awaited, the opportunity to achieve a particular dream. We must not miss our opportunities.

Each life is symbolized by a particular set of footprints in the snow. How wonderful and how freeing to know that we each offer something uniquely our own. We need never compete to be noticed. Each of us is guaranteed recognition for what we contribute, because it is offered by us alone.

Envy eats at us; it interferes with all of our interactions. It possesses all of our thoughts, caging us, denying us the freedom to achieve that can be ours.

I will look with love on my sisters. I will free them and myself to be all we are capable of becoming.

—from *Each Day a New Beginning*

May 22

Grace is when we notice the near-misses we survived instead of the wishes that didn't come true.

—NANCY HULL-MAST

We all have stories about the harrowing past: the times we woke up not knowing where we were, the open prescription bottle we couldn't remember emptying, the bashed-in fender, or the open front door of our home. How did we get from there to here? And why?

"There but for the grace of God . . ." is a saying that we come to appreciate when our mind finally clears. We were saved, many times. We have all read about people who weren't as lucky as we were. Curiously we wonder, Why me? Perhaps we should ponder, instead, what we can do with our lives now that we're here.

We have a unique contribution to make to our loved ones, or we wouldn't have "escaped." The next step is to listen to our inner voice for guidance. We have a job to do. It's time to get on with it.

It's no accident that I am here. I may not know what my job is today, but God will help me understand.

— from *A Woman's Spirit*

May 23

Love is an expression and assertion of self-esteem.
—AYN RAND

How easily we love others when we feel self-assured, when we're comfortable in our chosen work, with our families and friends, with our directions in life. But the way isn't always smooth, nor should it be, and for this we can thank God, our protector and mentor.

The challenges of a rough passage confront us when it's time to grow. Seldom do we cherish the growing, and yet the gifts promised by these challenges—the increased self-awareness, the heightened sensitivity to others, the greater humility—make every moment that lies ahead profoundly more personal.

Hindsight is convincing. The paradox is that the more we trip, but pick ourselves up and move ahead with determination, the more self-assured and thus loving we'll become.

—from *Worthy of Love*

May 24

One choice is all we ever need to make.

Because we feel bombarded by the changing circumstances of our lives, we tend to see them as far more complicated than they really are. Out of habit we try to make perfect decisions about many situations instantly. Our frustration and accompanying anxiety convinces us that every detail of life is critically serious. Of course, it isn't.

On the other hand, our daily experiences are important. Our experiences hold great purpose. We will discover what we need to know, and we will teach that which we have already learned if our hearts are open to the messages of the Spirit.

Our lives will be filled with joy and insight if we approach them with wonder, hope, and acceptance. The choice to see all experiences accordingly is the only choice that makes sense.

The choice to simplify or complicate my life is solely mine. Today will evolve as chosen.

—from *Daily Meditations for Practicing the* Course

May 25

My retirement hasn't been easy because it came earlier than I'd counted on.

Bud's story is not unusual. Many of us reading these pages were forced out of our jobs, and that situation can leave a lingering sense of self-doubt in our minds. But we can get beyond the pain of the experience with some willingness. Having a good support system around us will help. So will having a belief in spiritual "salvation."

We won't ever have all the answers we deserve regarding the circumstances in our lives. Over the years, many things happened that felt unfair or that we didn't understand. Depending on their nature, or how they affected us, we easily assimilated them or perhaps denied them. We generally got beyond them, at least. Some of our friends perhaps handled the mysteries in their lives more easily than ourselves. Might they have relied on a spiritual answer to those situations they didn't understand?

The point here is that some believe a spiritual perspective can always be adopted if confronted by an uncomfortable or frightening experience. Relying on a spiritual explanation might not change the experience, but it will change how we see it. And isn't that all that really matters?

I have experienced much that I hadn't counted on. Today may offer the same. I'll seek spiritual solace if necessary.

—from *Keepers of the Wisdom*

May 26

Taking a time-out will benefit everyone.

Reacting too quickly to any situation, grave or mundane, can lead us astray. Only by pausing first to hear God's suggestion can we be certain of doing the right thing or saying what's best. Somebody has to be willing to back away from an ugly conflict, or it can turn violent. Let's be the ones. The program has given us the tools, and we'll gain in the process. We'd never have won the war anyway.

Arguments are normal—healthy, even. We all see circumstances from unique perspectives; thus disagreements ensue. How we represent these perspectives is a sign of how much we have grown, and the opportunities for more growth will present themselves daily.

Learning that we have the choice to back away is powerful information. It makes peace possible.

I'll be quiet rather than argumentative today. The change will feel wonderfully peaceful.

—from *A Life of My Own*

May 27

Nothing gets old but your clothes. Only giving up and giving in makes you old.

—EVA WINES

Attitude is what makes us feel old. The number of years we've lived or the infirmity we suffer isn't nearly as important to our perception of age as is our attitude.

No doubt we know someone who has given up. We may have had bouts of depression and immobility too. We will experience whatever we choose daily. In the midst of a bout, it's not always easy to remember that we and only we have the power to discard it.

When we feel like giving up because we are tired and lonely, what might we do instead? Writing a note to someone we miss, calling a friend who seldom gets out or picking up a book we always meant to read takes us outside of ourselves. We'll find treasures there that we hadn't counted on. Our lives are only as gloomy as we make them.

I have control of my thinking today. I do every day, in fact. I'll adopt a positive attitude today.

—from *Keepers of the Wisdom*

May 28

Continuous effort—not strength or intelligence—is the key to unlocking our potential.

—LIANE CORDES

Perseverance may well be our greatest asset. As we forge ahead on a project, it loses its power over us. Our confidence and abilities grow in concert with our progress on the project, preparing us to tackle the next one too.

We have something special, uniquely our own to offer in this life. And we also have the potential to offer it successfully. However, we don't always realize our potential. Many of us stifled our development with fears of failure, low self-worth, assumed inadequacies. The past need plague us no longer.

Help is readily available for us to discover our capacities for success. Abilities stand ready to be tapped, goals and projects await our recognition. Any commitment we make to a task that draws our interest will be reinforced by God's commitment to our efforts. We have a partner. Our efforts are always doubled when we make them—truly make them.

I will not back away from a project today. I will persevere and find completion. I'll feel completed.

—from Each Day a New Beginning

May 29

I don't think you're suddenly going to begin to look at the world with new eyes when you're eighty if you haven't been doing it when you're thirty.

—JANICE CLARK

We are creatures of habit as evidenced by our getting stuck in old viewpoints long after they have quit serving us. However, that fact doesn't restrict us for all time. Anytime we want to cultivate a new idea, an alternative approach to a situation, we are free to do so. Janice may be right regarding some people she has known, but we are capable of freshening our perspective at any age.

We have all known some elderly men and women who have the spirit and enthusiasm of the very young. Unfortunately, we have also known the reverse. How sad to observe the forty- or fifty-year-old person who has quit living. Their whining belies their age. Who will we be? The choice is always available to us. And we can remake it as often as we wish.

What a relief to know that if we're old and resentful today, we still have the opportunity to be young and full of laughter tomorrow. We maybe can't do everything we used to do, but this decision is still in our power.

I will open my eyes to whatever I choose to see today. Yesterday's experiences have only the power I give them.

—from Keepers of the Wisdom

May 30

So often I have listened to everyone else's truth and tried to make it mine.

—LIANE CORDES

Being different from others was so painful in our youth. We wanted to belong, to look like our friends, to think like them, to be like them in every way. We wanted them to share our dreams and opinions. Rather than risk that they wouldn't, we mimicked them. Who were we? We seldom knew, because it depended on who we were with.

That is still a problem for many of us. Fortunately, our friends in this recovery program do not expect us to share their opinions unless they fit us too. Listening to another woman's truth honors her. Taking her truth as our own, when it isn't, dishonors both of us. This program teaches us respect if we are willing students. To be praised, rather than judged, for our integrity, even when it means we are different, is a refreshing and humbling experience.

I will listen to my truth today and respect everyone else's too. I am not here to judge, but to honor and love.

—from A Woman's Spirit

May 31

To give is to receive in kind.

Blasting the horn at a slow driver or yelling at a neighbor girl for running through our flowers may give us short-term satisfaction. We may feel righteous at the time, but when the moment has passed, we're generally a little ashamed. Why do we allow the ego so much power over our actions?

When we respond negatively to any experience, we have let the ego take charge. It loves to keep us agitated because then we stir up trouble. Our inner peace quickly disappears and we're completely at the mercy of the ego.

It helps some of us to think of the ego as an enemy. The contrast between the ego and the loving comfort the Holy Spirit offers is profound. The difference we would feel throughout our day-to-day experiences is, likewise, profound.

I am in charge of my thinking and my emotions. The choice to follow the ego or the Holy Spirit is mine today.

—from *Daily Meditations for Practicing the* Course

June

June 1

Find everyday reasons to dance.
—ELISABETH L.

Just being alive is reason enough to dance, if we ponder it for a moment. It's not an accident that we lived through sometimes terrifying experiences. Nor is it accidental that we are in our current setting. We are needed by our friends, our family, even the strangers among us. Let's cherish our opportunities to be in the presence of these others today.

Our lives are akin to a ballet. While learning the steps, we may stumble a bit, but the dance needs us all. Let's never assume another person isn't necessary to our own performance. If she is here, we need her.

How has this all happened? we wonder. How did I get here? Can I pull off my part? Our doubts need not hinder us if we remember that we got here with help; we'll fulfill our role with the same ready help.

I can kick up my heels today and know that I can dance. All I need to do is listen for the music.

—from *A Woman's Spirit*

June 2

Limited expectations yield only limited results.
—SUSAN LAURSON WILLIG

Schoolchildren perform according to the expectations their teachers have of them. Likewise, what we women achieve depends greatly on what we believe about ourselves, and too many of us have too little belief in ourselves. Perhaps we grew up in a negative household or had a nonsupportive marriage. But we contributed, too, in our negative self-assessment. The good news is that it no longer needs to control us.

We can boost our own performance by lifting our own expectations, even in the absence of support from others. It may not be easy, but each of us is capable of changing a negative self-image to a positive one. It takes commitment to the program, a serious relationship with our higher power, and the development of positive, healthy relationships with others.

It's true, we can't control other people in our lives. And we can't absolutely control the outcome of any particular situation. But we can control our own attitudes. Interestingly, when we've begun seeing ourselves as competent and capable, instead of inadequate, we find that other people and other situations become more to our liking, too.

I will be fair with myself. I can do what I need to do wherever I am today. Only I can hold myself down.

—from *Each Day a New Beginning*

June 3

We can learn to control our reactions.

Our bruised egos often push us to respond to other people in hurtful, thoughtless ways. Yet taking a moment to remember that everyone touched by an event has a different perspective helps us remain silent when our egos want to scream.

Deciding who is right and who is wrong wastes many precious moments every twenty-four hours. What we can learn in the program is that no one has to be right or wrong. We can decide, instead, that we'd rather be peaceful and let others have their own opinions.

We experience a rush of exhilarating freedom each time we back away from an unnecessary confrontation. The first few times we back away we may be uncomfortable, because arguing had become our habit. But we can make a habit too of not arguing. Serenity and empowerment will be the rewards.

No one makes me argue. I have chosen to. Today I will be quiet and peaceful and let others have their own opinions.

—from *A Life of My Own*

June 4

*Every artist dips his brush in his own soul, and
paints his own nature into his pictures.*

—HENRY WARD BEECHER

Our perception of any experience, even the smallest detail
of an ordinary event, is quite exceptional. No other person
will share our particular vision. Frequently that results in
arguments. The need to be right is a common affliction. If
only we could appreciate the richness of sharing and combining our views.

Because of our age, we may assume we have more wisdom than others. On occasion, we will. However, we have
something to learn from all souls who cross our path, or
they wouldn't be there. Understanding this is real wisdom.

What a dull world this would be if we all shared the
same perception of every event. There would be nothing to
discuss, no opportunity to expand our minds, no reason
to interact at all. Instead we are blessed with opportunities
for conflict and growth, the deepening of relationships
and character development, choices, and decisions. All because we each see what we see.

*How I see an experience today is unique but neither right nor
wrong. I will remember the same holds true for all my friends, too.*

—from *Keepers of the Wisdom*

June 5

Seek to know peace, nothing more.

When we're in conflict, we cry out for detailed solutions to our problems. We become apprehensive when we are unable to imagine what the situation needs. We fret and analyze and ask other people's opinions, but we still worry. Generally we assume a complicated answer is necessary.

The *Course* suggests we are making things too hard for ourselves. No matter what we think, we seldom need long, drawn-out solutions. We don't need the collective advice of many people. We don't need to seek one specific answer through prayer. We need peace; within it, miraculously, lie all answers.

The blessing for us is that peace is always available. It's never more than an instant away. In the quiet spaces of our minds, it waits to be called. Searching our minds for complex solutions to daily problems will never provide the answers we deserve. Seeking to know nothing but peace will always satisfy us.

The answers I seek are seldom where I look. I'll try being quiet today.

—from *Daily Meditations for Practicing the* Course

June 6

Love itself is not an act of will, but sometimes I need the force of my volition to break with my habitual responses and pass along the love already here.

—HUGH PRATHER

The familiarity of isolation is both haunting and inviting. In our separateness we contemplate the joys of shared hours with others while seeking the freedom from the pain that likewise hovers on the heels of intimate relationships. The question eternally whispering around our souls is, "Do I dare let you in, to share my space, to know my heart's longing, to feel my fears?" Only when we trust to say yes will we find the peace our souls long for.

Passage through the doors that separate us frees us to change, to grow, to love ourselves and others. We must plant our feet in the soil of shared lives to quiet our longing.

—from *Worthy of Love*

June 7

I must be prepared before the crisis comes.
—RUTH HUMLECKER

Being prepared for a crisis may seem like a negative out-look to some. After all, if we expect trouble, won't we get it? However, there is another way to think about prepara-tion: it is a chance to make sure the tools of the program are easily accessible and familiar through use.

For example, one valuable tool is available when we give our lives and will to God. We can handle any situation if we let our Higher Power help carry our burdens. Another valuable tool is communicating regularly with a sponsor. We can avoid many disasters when we seek her advice, since her thinking is often clearer than our own.

Many crises result from our attempts to force other people to live according to our rules. Becoming willing, through the broad application of Step One, to accept our powerlessness over everybody else saves us from many con-flicts. Unchecked conflicts are the stuff that crises are often made of.

The best preparation, of course, is believing that we'll never be given more than we can handle.

I am prepared to handle whatever comes to me today. The pro-gram will see me through every detail of my life.

—from *A Woman's Spirit*

June 8

I have found that sitting in a place where you have never sat before can be inspiring.

—DODIE SMITH

Repeatedly, today and every day, we will be in new situations, new settings with old friends, and old settings and situations with new friends. Each instance is fresh, unlike all the times before. And inspiration can accompany each moment, if we but recognize how special it is.

"We will never pass this way again," so the song says, which heightens the meaning of each encounter, every experience. Acknowledging that something can be gained each step along the way invites inspiration.

Inspiration moves us to new heights. We will be called to step beyond our present boundaries. Maybe today. Whenever the inspiration catches our attention, we can trust its invitation; we are ready for the challenge it offers. We need not let our narrow, personal expectations of an experience, a new situation perhaps, prevent us from being open to all the dynamic possibilities it offers.

I must be willing to let my whole self be moved, inspired. I must be willing to let each moment I experience be the only moment getting my attention.

—from *Each Day a New Beginning*

June 9

*Surrendering to God's caring plan eases our
walk today.*

When first introduced to the idea that a Higher Power is in
charge of our lives, the lives of our loved ones, and all the
situations we've struggled so hard to control, we balk. We
don't want to turn over the reins to anyone. After all, how
can we be certain our loved ones will stop drinking if we
quit pleading? Or who is going to make sure the children
don't get into drugs if we aren't nagging them about their
friends and their whereabouts all the time?

How lucky we are to have discovered, at last, the peace
that comes with surrendering. There is a plan for our lives.
There is a plan for our companion's life too. And for our
friends' and associates' lives. No one of us has been left
out of the divine plan. But we couldn't see this before. We
were too intent on trying to run lives as though we were
all-powerful. Now we can breathe easier, knowing God
will take care of all those people we tried to manage but
couldn't.

*As Step Three suggests, I will turn my will and my life over to God
today and enjoy these twenty-four hours.*

—from *A Life of My Own*

June 10

I've lost so many people in my life: my only brother, my husband, one child, a sister, her husband, and their son. Being spiritual has helped me handle all that.

Anything we have to handle, whether a monumental tragedy or a simple loss, is made easier if we believe that a Power greater than ourselves is watching over us. Some among our group of seniors have always known this. A few of us have not accepted this idea yet, perhaps. Our families of origin, along with teachers and peer groups, influenced our belief systems, and changing it doesn't come so easy the older we get.

If we aren't feeling peaceful on a daily basis, if we are fearful or full of dread about what the future holds, we might find relief in a change in perspective. That's all a belief system is, in fact. It's a perspective that explains how we see the world. If we struggle to handle the uncertainties of this changing world, or if we feel overwhelmed by what's expected of us, deciding to look at our experiences in a new way makes sense.

Maybe you think you can't change your mind at this late date. But that's not true. The one thing we can always change, regardless of how old we are, is what we hold in our minds. No one has the power to put an idea there but ourselves. Is it time to make a change?

Do I feel peaceful and unafraid today? I can with a change of mind.

—from *Keepers of the Wisdom*

June 11

Unconditional love means total acceptance, free of all judgment.

Our judgments of other people may be blatant or subtle. When our judgments are blatant, we can recognize them, know that we aren't loving unconditionally, and consciously focus on letting the judgments go. More often, however, our thoughts are subtle and so much harder to let go of. But letting go is a goal we can strive for. Every experience with another person allows us an opportunity to love unconditionally, free of judgment.

Our judgments of others generally reflect how we feel about ourselves at the time. When we are in tune with our spiritual center and feeling confident, we are comfortable with others too. Going within ourselves is a tool we can use for getting free of our judgments. When they begin to shadow our thoughts, we can go within and find God and freedom.

My judgment of others is a barometer of how close I am to my Higher Power today. Prayer will help me love others and myself.

—from *A Life of My Own*

June 12

Occupation is essential.

—VIRGINIA WOOLF

Having desires, setting goals, and achieving them are necessary to our fulfillment. There is purpose to our lives, even when we can't clearly see our direction, even when we doubt our abilities to contribute. Let us continue to respond to our opportunities.

Many of us experienced the clouds of inaction in earlier periods . . . waiting, waiting, waiting, hoping our circumstances would change, even praying they would, but taking no responsibility for changing what was in our power. Inaction caged us. Stripped of power, life held little or no meaning. However, we've been given another chance. The program has changed our lives. We have a reason for living, each day, even the days we feel hopeless and worthless.

Maybe we are without a goal at this time. Perhaps the guidance is not catching our attention. We can become quiet with ourselves and let our daydreams act as indicators. We have something essential to do, and we are being given all the chances we'll need to fulfill our purpose. We can trust in our worth, our necessity to others.

I will remember, the program came to me. I must have a part to play. I will look and listen for my opportunities today.

—from *Each Day a New Beginning*

June 13

Every relationship is a teacher. If I don't learn the lesson, the teacher will come back.
—BRENDA M. SCHAEFFER

We get as many chances as we need to master the lessons destined for us in this life. That's good. It removes some of the anxiety about not getting everything right the first time. While it may not be easy to admit we are relearning an old lesson, the women who share our experiences in recovery understand. And there is no shame attached, except that which we haven't yet learned to shed.

There is a positive way to meet the return of a familiar lesson. We must be willing to give it a try once again. Then we need to have faith that we're ready to make progress.

Life is relationship. We can't avoid it. We can learn to love and to accept love through relationships. We can know forgiveness through them too. Mastering these lessons is all our Higher Power hopes for us.

I am a willing student today. I will expect an important lesson from every relationship.

—from *A Woman's Spirit*

June 14

To forgive, to heal, to love is why we're here.

We want to believe there is a grand design for our lives. Many of us believe that God needs us and us alone to handle a particular job. If that brings us peace and security, it's worth believing. But it might be simpler to believe that God just wants us to love each other. According to the *Course,* our careers or the tasks we're working on are not as important as how we treat the people we meet each day.

It is never wrong to do whatever work we're doing to the best of our ability. It may be that no other person can do it quite as successfully. We all hope to end up doing work we can enjoy and that contributes to the well-being of others. But at the very least, we can still contribute to the well-being of others by treating them lovingly.

Believing that we are here, now, for the sole purpose of loving others means we can all do an excellent job, no matter our age, our gender, or race; no matter our present livelihood or our dreams for the future.

Today I can treat others with grace and respect.

—from *Daily Meditations for Practicing the* Course

June 15

*The most important thing I've learned in life is to
love others and accept their love in return.*

—JIM BURNS

After decades of living and learning, is love really our most important lesson? Perhaps we doubt this. Whatever trade or profession we mastered provided well for us and our families. Surely education counted. And what of the thousands of simple tasks like driving a car, riding a bike, cooking a meal, balancing the checkbook? The list can go on endlessly. Let's not discard anything that we have learned as without value. In fact, every example we can think of has played its part. The point here is that *how* we did our tasks, regardless of their significance, is what really matters. Doing anything, whether great or small, with a mean heart leaves its mark. The converse is likewise true.

How does love really enter into the ordinary activities that engage us? Easy. When someone pulls in front of us in traffic, we can bless them. The snotty clerk at the grocery needs a smile. The friend who whines about her misfortunes deserves a hug, perhaps. We can refuse to offer anything but love in every circumstance. It may seem impossible; after all, there are so many situations and people who irritate us. But giving only love changes each person and every situation. And the one who is changed most of all is ourself.

Knowing that I can change any situation by what I bring to it thrills me. Today will be a test of my skill.

—from *Keepers of the Wisdom*

June 16

*Each moment of these twenty-four hours is unique
and will never come again.*

We can anticipate the day we have awakened to with a feeling of promise or dread. There will be situations, no doubt, that we'd rather not face. Petty irritations may shadow us part of the day, but most likely we'll find a few circumstances to laugh over. We will find more of these circumstances if we so choose. The attitude we have today will determine the quality of our day.

If only we knew how many days we were guaranteed, it might not matter so much what we did with just one of them. But we don't know. These twenty-four hours we awakened to today are ours to make the most of. And we can make each one of them pleasant and memorable, or very miserable. Letting someone else's behavior determine how we experience our own day can be disastrous. We know this from the pain we had in our lives prior to finding this program.

I will find as much joy in today as I want to find. I will try to remember that each moment is sacred and full of promise.

—from *A Life of My Own*

June 17

Give to the world the best you have, and the best will come back to you.

—MADELINE BRIDGE

We do reap, in some measure, at some time, what we sow. Our respect for others will result in kind. Our love expressed will return tenfold. The kindness we greet others with will ease their relations with us. We get from others what we give, if not at this time and place, at another. We can be certain that our best efforts toward others do not go unnoticed. And we can measure our due by what we give.

A major element of our recovery is the focus we place on our behavior, the seriousness with which we tackle our inventories. We can look at ourselves and how we reach out and act toward others; it is a far cry from where we were before entering this program. Most of us obsessed on "What he did to me," or "What she said." And then returned their actions in kind.

How thrilling is the knowledge that we can invite loving behavior by giving it! We have a great deal of control over the ebb and flow of our lives. In every instance we can control our behavior. Thus never should we be surprised about the conditions of our lives.

What goes around comes around. I will look for the opportunities to be kind and feel the results.

—from *Each Day a New Beginning*

June 18

We can't create transformational spiritual experiences by sheer will, but we can encourage them by being open to them.

—VERONICA RAY

How does one define a spiritual experience? Perhaps the most we can say is that we know, oftentimes very subtly, that something wonderful has happened. We suddenly sense that we are safe, in good hands, and the pain or turmoil of our lives is passing.

Our spiritual guide or our Higher Power is always with us, always trying to help us, always acting as a protector and teacher. Unfortunately, many of us can't quiet our minds enough to capture the essence of God's presence in all our experiences, the mundane as well as the obviously significant. Making the Second Step of this program the foundation for daily living opens us to the myriad possibilities for the spiritual experiences we seek. "Coming to believe" is right next to "believing." Believing is next to knowing.

My life is on a spiritual plane. God's presence, thus my safety, is as close as my next thought today.

—from *A Woman's Spirit*

June 19

Extending love to you heals me.

Too often we hold back, waiting for someone else to give to us before we respond. Simply reacting to life grows tiresome, however. To risk acting first offers us real freedom. Until we try it, we can't imagine how empowering it is.

All of us think we are in a state of need. We think we need more money, more possessions, more beauty, or more friends. If only we had enough, our problems would dissolve. The paradox is that whatever we think we lack is supplied when we give, and so get, more love.

We can heal the lack we feel in only one way: by extending ourselves lovingly, to others. We may hesitate to extend ourselves because we fear we're unworthy of others. What could we possibly have done that they'd want?

It's time for suspending our fears and disbelief. It's time for daring to love.

I yearn to be healed. On any day my soul aches, I can soothe it by offering love. Today I'll find an opportunity.

—from *Daily Meditations for Practicing the* Course

June 20

... love grows by service.
—CHARLOTTE PERKINS GILMAN

When we shower someone special with much-needed attention, or maybe flowers, or run an errand for a friend, or volunteer to do a favor for an unnamed person, we benefit in many ways. We're appreciated; we feel good about our own behavior, and we've tightened the connection to another person that fosters personal human development.

Most of us long for more signs of love from one another. Yet we fail to understand that our own expression of love to that special someone will release the love we long to feel.

Love multiplies with frequency of expression, whether stranger to stranger, friend to friend, lover to lover, parent to child; and everyone is the beneficiary.

Love's expression spontaneously generates more of itself, thus promising each of us what we long for.

—from *Worthy of Love*

June 21

When I remember to listen and savor another's experience as valuable and sacred, I touch a sense of mystery.

—RITA CASEY

As much as we may want to deny it, few of us are truly attentive listeners. We try to listen. We even work hard to keep our own obsessive thoughts quiet. But turning our entire attention to a friend in need is a trait we may never perfect. Even so, listening is a worthy pursuit, because very frequently God's wisdom comes to us through another person's words.

Our intimate moments with another soul are never accidental or inconsequential. We are like dancers in a ballet. Each of our movements has its complement in another's movement. We have been drawn together to complete the story for one another. And it's imperative to hear another's words if we are to fulfill our very special role. We can know God's will if we listen closely to the words of others.

We should remember that God is present always in our friends with the message our souls await.

Dear God, help me listen today to your message as it is expressed through my friends.

—from *A Woman's Spirit*

June 22

When action grows unprofitable, gather information; when information grows unprofitable, sleep.
—URSULA K. LE GUIN

Sometimes we need to turn away from what's troubling us. Turn it over, says the Third Step. Hanging on to a situation for which no solution is immediately apparent only exaggerates the situation. It is often said the solution to any problem lies within. However, turning the problem over and over in our minds keeps our attention on the outer appearance, not the inner solution.

Rest, meditation, quiet attention to other matters, other persons, opens the way for God to reveal the solution. Every problem can be resolved. And no answer is ever withheld for long. We need to be open to it, though. We need to step away from our ego, outside of the problem and then listen fully to the words of friends, to the words that rise from our own hearts. Too much thinking, incessant analyzing, will keep any problem a problem.

I will rest from my thoughts. I will give my attention wholly to the present. Therein will come the solution, and when least expected.

—from *Each Day a New Beginning*

June 23

❧

Gratitude enhances all blessings.

Sometimes we just don't feel grateful. We struggle to get out of bed. Begrudgingly, we go to work. Smiling at other people is an effort we can barely make. It's hard to imagine we ever felt grateful or enthusiastic about our lives.

How do we break loose from a negative state of mind? First, we need to remember that whatever we harbor in the mind is what we put there. And with concentrated effort we can be rid of it. Second, making a list of all the blessings we can see in our lives, at this moment, will assure us of God's love. Sometimes we forget that we are here purposefully. And when that happens, it is so easy to lose our enthusiasm. That's normal, so let's not fret for long about it. Instead, let's recapture the proper frame of mind once again by remembering we have a purpose and counting our blessings.

No matter how uninspired I feel, I will remember that God has a plan for me and has blessed me. This will free me from the doldrums.

—from *A Life of My Own*

June 24

Some things we think are bad may be good.
—HARRY BARTHOLOMEW

Making hasty judgments about people can be detrimental. We quickly decide if an invitation to dinner is worth our time, or maybe we pass up an opportunity to engage in a book club or get acquainted with a prospective friend simply because we are a bit fearful. Does it really make sense to so quickly dispense with the people or the possibilities that beckon when we have so much time to spare?

While it is true that some opportunities may not be good, we can't make educated judgments about anything without at least a modicum of exposure. It's *by design* that we are still here, in this life, in these bodies. Perhaps we should be more open and trust the Grand Designer. Quietly seeking our inner voice will tell us what to do.

No doubt we have all regretted passing up opportunities after hearing of another's experiences with them. That doesn't have to be the standard for our lives, though. Careful contemplation coupled with some quiet meditation will always guide us appropriately. Taking the time to fully consider an option allows us to cull the good from the bad.

I don't have to accept every invitation that comes my way, but I can be open to new options.

—from *Keepers of the Wisdom*

June 25

Acknowledging our defects is the first step in giving them up.

Keeping track of the shortcomings of other people is second nature to us. Many of us have been obsessed, in fact, with how others live their lives. Since we're all different, it goes without saying that we behave differently, we think differently, and we perform our jobs differently. What's more, our values, even when similar, manifest always in slightly different ways. Thus we have multiple opportunities for judging others.

But this program is about keeping the attention on us, instead. It's our behavior, our character defects, and our lives that we have some control over. We have caused problems for ourselves many times, because we haven't been as willing to see our own defects as we have been to see the defects of others. There is no time like the present for changing our focus.

I will keep my eyes on myself today. I realize I am not without defects. But I can change mine.

—from *A Life of My Own*

June 26

❦

... The present enshrines the past.
—SIMONE DE BEAUVOIR

Each of our lives is a multitude of interconnecting pieces, not unlike a mosaic. What has gone before, what will come today, are at once and always entwined. The past has done its part, never to be erased. The present is always a compromise.

In months and years gone by, perhaps we anticipated the days with dread. Fearing the worst, often we found it; we generally find that which we fear. But we can influence the mosaic our experiences create. The contribution today makes to our mosaic can lighten its shade, can heighten its contrast, can make bold its design.

What faces us today? A job we enjoy or one we fear? Growing pains of our children? Loneliness? How we move through the minutes, the hours, influences our perception of future minutes and hours.

No moment is inviolate. Every moment is part of the whole that we are creating. We are artists. We create our present from influences of our past.

I will go forth today; I will anticipate goodness. I will create the kind of moments that will add beauty to my mosaic.

—from *Each Day a New Beginning*

June 27

⊷

We need to let the old go, so the new can emerge.
—PEGGY BASSETT

When we first entered the program, we heard the saying, "One door must close before another can open." That baffled us, even while it gave us comfort. It helped that women we looked up to found solace in the slogan. Their experiences, shared in the meetings, taught us understanding. Each time we fought against a changing condition, someone we admired was able to remind us of its value.

Now we are the truth-bearers for the newcomers. Over time we have come to believe that every experience has special meaning. When something new begins to tap us on the shoulder, that's our cue to let something else go. Newcomers need our demonstration of how it works. No doubt, before this day or this week has passed, we'll each have an opportunity to close one door and open another. Let's make sure we share what we learn with someone else.

I am someone's teacher today. I will not fight circumstances that are changing, but accept that their passing is my opportunity.

—from *A Woman's Spirit*

June 28

Sharing our experiences heightens our joy and lessens our pain.

Not letting other people know what's troubling us causes the problem to trouble us even more. "Secrets keep us stuck," say the wise ones on our journey.

Sharing what's on our minds with a friend or sponsor gives that person an opportunity to help us develop a better perspective. On the other hand, staying isolated with our worries exaggerates them.

Staying isolated with our joys isn't helpful either. It minimizes them, thus cheating us out of feeling their full thrill. We deserve joy in our lives—lots of it—because we will have our full measure of pain. Perhaps we fear others will criticize us for being braggarts if we sing forth our joy. But our real friends will sing right along with us. Our joys are deserved; they offset our trials. Telling others about both will let all our experiences count for something.

I will remain open to my friends today, sharing both my worries and my joys.

—from *A Life of My Own*

June 29

And what a delight it is to make friends with
someone you have despised!

—COLETTE

What does it mean to say we "despise" someone? Usually it means that we have invested a lot of energy in negative feelings; it means that we have let ourselves care deeply about someone. We would never say we "despised" someone who wasn't important to us. Why have we chosen to let negative feelings occupy so much of our hearts?

Sometimes, in the past, that negative energy became almost an obsession, consuming our time, gnawing at our self-esteem. But in recovery there comes a moment of lightning change; a moment of release from the bonds of obsession. The other person is, after all, just another person—a seeker, like ourselves. And, since we cared enough to devote our time and energies to disliking her, she is probably someone who would be rewarding to know.

Recovery has given us the opportunity to turn over many negative feelings, to discover that "friend" and "enemy" can be two sides of the same person.

Today, I will look into my heart and see whether I am clinging to obsessive concerns with other people. I will resolve to let them go.

—from *Each Day a New Beginning*

June 30

A crisis is only a turning point.
—ANNE LINDTHORST

The sting is removed from a crisis when we accept it as a turning point. Our lives have been full of turning points. A moment's reflection brings to mind crises that moved us to far better places. For instance, we may not have counted on finding sobriety and this program of recovery, but a significant crisis delivered us here.

Because we remember how frightening a crisis can be, let's make an effort to help our sisters gain a healthier perspective on the turning points in their lives. When we're in a rocking boat, it's not easy to remember that a storm ushers in clear skies. Sharing this information with our struggling sisters keeps us from forgetting it too.

With enough faith, we can look forward to the lessons and growth experiences life offers. We'll ever doubt their contribution to our developing nature.

I need not fear a troubling situation today. It is offering me a lesson I am ready to learn.

—from *A Woman's Spirit*

July

July 1

God has given each of us a special gift.

How often we wake up doubting ourselves depends on how caught we are in the grasp of the ego. Some days going to work seems overwhelming. Handling difficult children or mending fences with a parent gives us fits of anxiety. Obviously we have forgotten the Holy Spirit. We never experience these pangs of uncertainty when we have sought Its help.

If only we could remember that we are exactly where our "services" are needed every single minute. And what are the services? Simply to listen to others with our hearts, and respond with love. No matter where we are or what occupation we have, our task is the same.

We complicate our experiences so much, always trying to figure out the right solution. There is only one solution for everything! We can give up the angst, the need to be right, the worry over outcomes. None of it matters. If we have forgiveness and love in our hearts, we are fulfilling our purpose.

My participation in today's events will reflect the love the Holy Spirit has given me.

—from *Daily Meditations for Practicing the* Course

July 2

I visualize the things I'd like to do and they fall into place.

—FRAN COYNE

The power of visualization is a bit mysterious, isn't it? How it works, perhaps, isn't so important. That it does work is attested to by many. Athletes often credit their superior performance to the power of visualization. Golfers commonly talk about imagining their ball's trajectory before every shot. Therapists tell clients to "see" themselves calmly handling situations prior to the actual circumstance.

Today may be a good time to experiment with this tool. Consider something you'd like to do. Perhaps take a trip, plant a garden, paint a picture, or organize the hundreds of photographs that have accumulated over the years. Take a few quiet moments to "observe" yourself getting organized and a few more moments "watching" yourself follow through with the activity. The meditative process acts as a motivator, pushing us forward into the activity. It also seems to help ready us for the arising opportunities that will enhance the actual pursuit.

We can't rationally explain how this process works. But do we need to? Books are filled with examples of success. Rather than doubt the possibility of our success with any activity that appeals to us, let's try visualization first. It's probable that we can add our stories of success to all the others.

I'll close my eyes and imagine what I want to do next. That's the first step to success.

—from *Keepers of the Wisdom*

July 3

*If we think too much, we hinder our understanding
and our progress.*

Step Eleven suggests that we'll improve our conscious contact with God if we pray and meditate. The meditation
part is particularly important. It's the avenue between us
and our Higher Power's guidance. Quieting our minds of
our obsession with what other people are doing isn't always easy. But it's there, in the quiet, that we'll feel God's
guidance, God's message, God's comfort.

Having busy minds isn't unusual. Nor is it accidental.
Our minds are full because we fill them. If we want quiet
minds in order to know God better, we must empty them.

God answers our prayers in the quiet spaces of our
minds. Let's listen.

*I will clear my mind today so God can reach me with what I need
to know.*

—from *A Life of My Own*

July 4

*Like an old gold-panning prospector, you must
resign yourself to digging up a lot of sand from
which you will later patiently wash out a few
minute particles of gold ore.*

—DOROTHY BRYANT

Sometimes we feel buried in sand, blocked, clogged, unable to move. Then we must remember that we are not alone. Help is at hand, if only we will ask for it. If we invoke our higher power, our source of spiritual strength can help us to believe that there is gold somewhere in all this sand, and that the sand itself is useful.

No one and no thing is good all the time. Let us remember that if we expect nothing but gold, we are distorting life, getting in our own way. We don't want to falsify the texture of our lives; the homespun quality helps us to appreciate the gold when it appears.

I will find some gold among the sand, today.

—from *Each Day a New Beginning*

July 5

*Every ending is part of a beginning. Every loss is
part of an emptiness that can be filled with newness.*
—JAN LLOYD

The door that is closing today may fill us with dread; however, we can find relief when we recall other endings that unexpectedly led to new friendships, better jobs, wonderful opportunities.

Life is a process. Every event in our lives is connected to what has gone before and what will come after. There are no real endings; there are only new opportunities for growth and change. For most of us it's a matter of changing our perspective. The difference is subtle yet extremely powerful, and our lives will never feel the same.

I look forward to these twenty-four hours! I can be glad for everything that comes to me, trusting in its blessing.

—from *A Woman's Spirit*

July 6

Holy relationships await us.

We can't exist without relationships. We mingle with others throughout the day—co-workers, children, spouses, parents, friends. We are thrown together with strangers on the subway, neighbors at the grocery store, and advertisers at company meetings. Since we don't live secluded from others, we have to get along somehow. But how? That's one of our biggest concerns.

The *Course* says there is only one way to get along with others. It's the same formula whether we love or dislike the person. We need to seek a holy perspective of the relationship we share. We need God's help to see that person and ourselves in a circle of light and love. Our feelings will be changed accordingly—every time.

Even the most troubling individual will not disturb our inner peace if we seek to see our coming together as holy. This may sound impossible, or at least improbable, but it's true nonetheless. Testing this idea will dispel our doubts.

Today is a good day for experiments. I will seek the holy in even the ordinary.

—from *Daily Meditations for Practicing the* Course

July 7

You have to feel that you make a difference.
—MONTY CRALLEY

Most of us made our marks in careers or as homemakers. We probably had daily evidence from our bosses, customers, spouses, or children that what we did mattered. Now the feedback is less frequent. There may even be days when we have no contact with others. The phone doesn't ring. The mail contains only circulars deserving of the trash can. Even television may not engage our thoughts. On those days we have to work a little harder to believe that we still matter.

Richard Bach, the author of *Illusions,* says that if we are still alive, we haven't yet fulfilled our mission. We still matter. Seems funny that an idea so simple can be so meaningful, but it is if we believe it.

We can decide to believe whatever makes us happiest. It will certainly be true for most of us that believing we count will give us greater comfort than thinking we don't. Why would we want to make our lives any harder? Don't we deserve to feel good? Of course we do. Let's go for it.

I do make a difference. With every breath I take I add something to the universe. This is God's promise to me.

—from *Keepers of the Wisdom*

July 8

God does not require that we be successful, only that we be faithful.

—MOTHER TERESA

It's probable we have never equated success with faith. Being successful meant accomplishing worthy goals and receiving the expected praise. We may have even considered that relying on faith to help us was a cop-out. Fortunately, so much about how we interpret life has changed since joining this journey through recovery.

In Step Three we learn that God wants us to have faith. We are coming to see, in fact, that acting as if we have faith begins to feel like faith. Coming to believe that God's only expectation is that we turn within for guidance makes every circumstance far less threatening.

Practicing faith promises that we will begin to feel successful in all our experiences because we are walking through them peacefully, trusting fully that God is at hand. Believing in God, being truly faithful, can be the greatest success of our lives.

I can be faith-filled today if I turn my life and my will over to the care of God. I will remind myself of this every time I get in the "driver's seat."

—from *A Woman's Spirit*

July 9

Friendship means more to me than money. Pass on friendship. I'd rather be on my death bed with a friend than with a million dollars.

—VIOLET HENSLEY

How good a friend have we been over the years? It took effort, patience, and willingness. It required that we put another's needs before our own, sometimes. It meant saying we were sorry and taking responsibility for all of our actions, even those we'd rather have forgotten. It meant being honest.

Violet's words speak volumes. We all have come to know loneliness in our advancing years. Losing spouses and any number of acquaintances has become common to us. And with each passing friend, we find ourselves closer to our own end. Having a friend to share the hours with, to share our memories and remaining dreams with, to share both laughter and tears with, makes every moment that remains of our lives more poignant, more purposeful.

If our friends are few, there is action we can take. Organizations of all kinds need us. So do schools and churches. People just like ourselves live behind thousands of closed doors. Let's seek someone out if we're alone today.

I am only as lonely as I want to be today. I can make the first move toward someone else.

—from Keepers of the Wisdom

July 10

There are as many ways to live and grow as there are people. Our own ways are the only ways that should matter to us.

—EVELYN MANDEL

Wanting to control other people, to make them live as we'd have them live, makes the attainment of serenity impossible. And serenity is the goal we are seeking in this recovery program, in this life.

We are each powerless over others, which relieves us of a great burden. Controlling our own behavior is a big enough job. Learning to behave responsibly takes practice. Most of us in this recovery program have behaved irresponsibly for much of our lives. Emotional immaturity is slow to depart, but every responsible action we take gives us the courage for another—and then another. Our own fulfillment is the by-product of the accumulation of our own responsible actions. Others' actions need not concern us.

Today, I will weigh my behavior carefully. Responsible behavior builds gladness of heart.

—from *Each Day a New Beginning*

July 11

When others upset us, we need to look in the mirror.

Every time we resent, or worse, hate, what another person is doing or saying, we need to acknowledge that we are the same. That's not easy. We don't want to own all that we are. In fact, that's the reason we see certain traits in others. We've denied they are our own by pushing them onto someone else and then judging that person. But our denial has now run its course. Adjusting to all that we are and forgiving our imperfections make it possible for us to honor others with forgiveness too. That's why we are here.

When we willingly see that we are here to understand and cherish forgiveness, we will feel neither fear nor anger when others upset us. We'll simply know that an opportunity to connect with another soul and celebrate our Oneness has presented itself.

School is always in session. At times, this may distress us, but we can be relieved instead. It means we have as many chances and as much time as it takes to grasp all that we are here to learn. What we miss today will come again tomorrow.

Keeping my mirror close by will teach me many things today.

—from *Daily Meditations for Practicing the* Course

July 12

A lesson exists in everything we experience.

It often seems ludicrous to believe that every situation involving us is by design. For instance, how could we have chosen to experience so closely and personally the disease of addiction? And why were we attracted to lovers who repeatedly abused us emotionally, if not physically? Lots of us absolutely intended to be good parents. So why did our children become substance abusers?

There are no adequate answers to these questions. We simply have to trust that what comes our way is meant for our ultimate good. Hindsight provides acceptance, if not always understanding.

Old-timers in this Twelve Step program tell us we are in the right place at the right time. It may sound crazy, but those whom we perceive wise seem to believe it. With time and experience, we'll come to trust their wisdom. We'll also come to value the lessons gained through today's experiences.

I will not fret over whatever is happening today; instead, I'll trust that today's circumstances will make me a wiser person.

—from *A Life of My Own*

July 13

The most important thing that was passed on to me by my parents was love. I tried to pass that on to my children, too.

—BEVERLY SHERMAN

Offering love to those who share our paths is the most important contribution any of us can make today. It was always our most important contribution, even though we generally thought our careers or homemaking roles were more important. Isn't it interesting that so few of us ever really understood what our *real purpose* was?

Some of us might wonder even now what's so important about passing on love. It's not that hard, is it? But honest reflection reveals how difficult loving others can actually be. To love unconditionally means we don't leave some people out and love only those who are easy to love. Passing on love means compassion and offering undivided attention to all the people accompanying us on our journey today. It means giving everybody the benefit of the doubt if we aren't in agreement with them. It means being willing to let others have their own opinions without trying to change them or judge them.

Loving others is more complex than many of us imagined. The good aspect of this is that we can stay busy learning to love for the rest of our lives. We'll never be done making this contribution to society. That's pretty exciting.

Am I ready to love everyone I meet today? I can become willing to embrace this purpose.

—from *Keepers of the Wisdom*

July 14

~○

Shifting perceptions changes us completely.

No situation looks quite the same to any two observers. We came to understand this through our willingness to listen to others and surrender the ego's insistence on being right. This is not the same as asking for a different perspective for ourselves, though. And this is what the *Course* suggests we do.

Some of us wonder how this can be. Surely, whatever we see is what is there. Right? Not necessarily. What we see is the absolute reflection of what our hearts are feeling. If it's love we're feeling, we'll see a situation that is hopeful and fulfilling. If it's fear, our vision will be profoundly clouded and our response will be agitated, angry, and full of attack.

We might liken our behavior to having a split personality. Who we appear to be one moment may not resemble who we'll become with a small shift in perception. This tiny act can result in a huge change. We quite likely wish we could have a loving perspective all the time. With a little effort, we can.

I can see however I choose today. How I act will follow accordingly.

—from *Daily Meditations for Practicing the* Course

July 15

It is impossible to overemphasize the immense need humans have to be really listened to, to be taken seriously, to be understood.

—PAUL TOURNIER, M.D.

We need assurance that our presence has value to the lives of those around us at home, work, and play. Our self-worth should not be solely tied to someone else's attention to us or love for us; however, our personal being is validated and thus enhanced each time we have evidence of being fully listened to.

Just as we hunger for attention and validation, so do the many people sharing our travels at this time. And sadly, we're rushing through our experiences not very attentive to either the events or the persons who have engaged our involvement.

The choice to slow down, to honor the flowers, the children, the loud and silent moments of the day, is ours. It's an expression of love for life, for ourselves and everyone we encounter if we take a moment to look and listen with our full being.

Each aspect of life is enriched when honored by a listening heart. Let's cherish the golden rule.

—from *Worthy of Love*

July 16

Seldom will we remember next week what bothers us so much today.

We'll have many opportunities to worry before this day ends. Some situations may even be grave. Perhaps a child gets picked up on a drunk-driving charge or a spouse loses another job because of absenteeism. It's not easy to shrug our shoulders when our loved one's troubles infringe on our lives. But the program will help us, and we'll come to understand that shrugging our shoulders doesn't mean we don't care. Rather, it means we are choosing not to do for other people what they must do for themselves.

Life is a process that includes problems that can't always be easily resolved. How refreshing to learn that we don't have to resolve every conflict. We can simply let conflicts be and focus on peaceful images and think loving thoughts instead. We can be certain that we won't remember most of today's troubles tomorrow unless we want to.

Because I used to worry far too much, life wasn't as fun as I'm now capable of making it. Today won't be a repeat of the old days. No matter what happens, I need not worry. God will take care of me.

—from *A Life of My Own*

July 17

*Fear is only an illusion. It is the illusion that
creates the feeling of separateness—the false sense
of isolation that exists only in your imagination.*
—JERALDINE SAUNDERS

We are one. We are connected, interdependent parts of the whole. We are not separate from each other except in the mind, in our false understanding of reality. As we come to understand our connectedness, our need for one another to complete the whole of creation, our fears will die.

It is often said we learn who we really are by closely observing our behavior toward the people in our lives. We meet ourselves in those others. They are our reflections. They are, perhaps, parts we ourselves have not yet learned to love. The program's message is to trust, to have faith; our higher power is in control. We are faced with no person, no situation too big to handle if we trust the program, if we remember the connections among us all.

I will look around today at others, with knowledge of our oneness. Fearing not, I will smile upon the wholeness of life.

—from *Each Day a New Beginning*

July 18

*It is important that we plan for the future,
imperative that we accept an outcome unplanned.*
—MOLLY MCDONALD

We sometimes feel confused over how to live just one day at a time while making strategic plans for the future. It seems contradictory to try to do both. Yet that is what a healthy recovery means.

Goals help direct our attention. They give us needed focus. They give us enthusiasm for making the most of our recovery. But just as we need goals to strengthen our resolve to move forward, we need willingness to let God be involved in our effort and, even more important, in charge of the outcome. God's role and ours, though related, are in fact quite separate. In our rush to move forward we sometimes forget to turn over the reins when our part is done.

We are learning the joys of living one day at a time. We are letting God be responsible for the outcomes of our endeavors. Each day in recovery gives us more time to practice doing only what we need to do and leaving the rest in God's hands.

I must let God take charge of the outcomes of my efforts today. If I do, I will be cared for in the most loving fashion.

—from *A Woman's Spirit*

July 19

Listening to a caring friend is one of the ways we hear God's message.

We think we listen, probably because we are in conversation with other people so often. But our own ongoing inner dialogue often shuts out much of what someone is saying. Whether at Twelve Step meetings or at lunch with a friend, we're preoccupied with the many people in our lives, or maybe our jobs, or an event we are organizing. Our minds get filled with the clutter of other times, other places, and we fail to hear the message at *this* single moment.

Peace will come to us when we slow down and quietly listen. When we remember that our friends are often the channel God relies on to reach us, we are eager to hear their words. Since seeking recovery, we have also become seekers of God's will. We may hear our next direction in a friend's suggestion today.

I will quietly listen to the loving words of my friends today.

—from *A Life of My Own*

July 20

❦

*I feel we have picked each other from the crowd
as fellow-travelers, for neither of us is to the other's
personality the end-all and the be-all.*

—JOANNA FIELD

We must look around at the people in our lives today, and know that we have something special to offer each of them, and they to us. We do travel separate paths together. We may need to learn tolerance; perhaps a friend's behavior pushes us to be more tolerant. Impatience may be our nemesis, and everywhere we turn are long lines and traffic jams. Our experiences with others aren't chance. Fellow travelers are carefully selected by the inner self, the spiritual guide who understands our needs in this life.

We are both the teachers and the pupils. We need both our friends and those we may label our enemies for what they can help us learn.

I will carefully look about me today with gladness at the travelers I've selected to learn from.

—from *Each Day a New Beginning*

July 21

I walked across an open field at winter's break as the sun danced on the last few drifts. I imagined my fears would melt one by one as I learned to love myself.

—LAUREL LEWIS

Fear is as familiar as our image in a mirror. Although we have resolved many of the fears that bound us to old behavior, our original fears may have been replaced by new ones. Why are there so many things to be afraid of? New friends, old relationships, careers, family history, tomorrow...

Acknowledging our fear is the first step to getting free of its control. Naming the fear puts us in charge. Remembering that we have a loving Higher Power who won't abandon us, even in the midst of our deepest fear, can help us get through too.

But loving our small, scared selves will be the most nurturing of all. Mothering ourselves, in the way we may have longed for mothering in our youth, will carry us through the most difficult times.

Fears are part of living. They are neither bad nor good; instead, they can teach us. They can help us learn to love more of ourselves.

I will welcome my fears today. They are my blueprint for who I am. God and I will comfort me with love.

—from A Woman's Spirit

July 22

The world does not have to change for me to be happy.

It's not easy to believe that we can be happy if we're in the middle of an unwanted divorce or nursing a terminally ill parent. Rearing children who are out of control is depressing too. Most of us need to look no further than our immediate surroundings to find a reason for unhappiness. It seems like denial when someone tells us the choice to be happy, in spite of circumstances, is easily made.

Looking beyond the contours of the events in our lives is an attainable skill. It doesn't mean our eyes don't see the painful details in this physical realm. Rather, it means we understand that the "material" isn't the actual substance of the spiritual, and it's the spiritual realm we truly seek to know. Our access to this realm lies within our minds. It takes nothing more than the sincere wish to see our circumstances differently to be able to do so. The Holy Spirit is our pathway.

The awful situations that may surround me today cannot hold me hostage. I can be happy if I seek the help of the Holy Spirit.

—from *Daily Meditations for Practicing the* Course

July 23

❧

I know I need something to do every day. It probably
doesn't even matter what it is.

—THELMA ELLIOTT

Being busy is what Thelma desires. That may not be true
for everyone. However, it's important that each of us rec-
ognizes what we do need. Taking an inventory of how
we're feeling and noting what we're doing will offer some
clues regarding our contentment or lack of it. If we aren't
fully satisfied, we need to make some changes.

But how do we know what to change if we're not as
happy as we'd hoped to be? Talking about our dreams
and disappointments with a friend will be enlightening
and a good first step. Deciding to change only one detail
of our lives at a time is a good decision, too. Seeking to
understand the way others have made their choices about
what to do makes sense also. It's not coincidental that
we're in communication with a particular group of people.
They are here as teachers. Assuredly we are instructing
them as well.

Making our lives matter, keeping them rich and interesting, appeals to us all. How we go about doing this varies
according to one's personality. What we can all be certain
of, however, is that it matters not what we do but how we
feel doing it. We can gauge this easily.

Am I content with my life today? If something is amiss, I'll talk
with a friend.

—from *Keepers of the Wisdom*

July 24

I can change only myself, but sometimes that is enough.

—RUTH HUMLECKER

Happiness is more fleeting for some of us than for others. We may ponder this notion but fail to grasp the reason. However, careful attention to how "the happy ones" go through life will enlighten us. We will note how seldom they complain about others' actions. We will discover their willingness to accept others as they are. We will see that their attention is generally on the positive aspects of people and circumstances rather than on the negative.

We can join the parade of "happy ones" by letting go of our need to change people and situations that disturb us. Even when we are certain other people are wrong, we can let go of controlling them. Doing this means changing ourselves, of course. But this is the one thing in life we do have control over.

I will change myself if I think something needs changing today!

—from *A Woman's Spirit*

July 25

I look in the mirror through the eyes of the child that was me.

—JUDY COLLINS

The child within each of us is fragile, but very much alive, and she interprets our experiences before we are even conscious of them. It is our child who may fear new places, unfamiliar people, strange situations. Our child needs nurturing, the kind she may not have received in the past. We can take her hand, coax her along, let her know she won't be abandoned. No new place, unfamiliar person, or strange situation need overwhelm her.

It's quite amazing the strength that comes to us when we nurture ourselves, when we acknowledge the scared child within and hold her, making her secure. We face nothing alone. Together, we can face anything.

I will take care of my child today and won't abandon her to face, alone, any of the experiences the day may bring.

—from Each Day a New Beginning

July 26

Remember the smallest blessings.

Blessings abound in our lives. Even when all we can see is the havoc the alcoholic has caused, we need to remember the tiny joys: the call from a friend, the smiles from strangers, the beauty of nature. It's so easy to fall into hopelessness when we focus all our attention on what the addict is doing despite our pleas.

We can cultivate a brighter outlook in much the same way we cultivate a garden. We can plant the seed of God's love in our minds every morning and water it throughout the day with tiny prayers of gratitude. If we do this, our hearts will be uplifted by nightfall. Making a practice of this will change us completely.

It may sound too simple at first, but the winners among us have learned how to feel happy even in the midst of conflict. They aren't privileged in any special way. We can have what they have with a little "gardening."

I deserve to feel good about my life today. I have many blessings that I take for granted. I'll think about them today, and my attitude will reflect my gratitude.

—from *A Life of My Own*

July 27

*Everything changes—but some things change
more slowly.*

—JANICE CLARK

Experience has taught us that change is inevitable. But getting used to this has seldom been easy, particularly if we liked how the circumstances of our lives were going. And then, of course, there were less comfortable situations that we prayed would change. Sometimes they did. Often they didn't, at least not on our timetable. That change is simply a fact of life is never more obvious than when we look at old photographs or sort through the memorabilia that children have left behind.

The physical changes that have occurred in most of us are often distressing. Did we honestly think we'd be agile and full of energy forever? The death of a loved one is one change that we all must confront, more frequently as the years slip by. No matter how many friends we have lost already, the next one is still difficult. Saying good-bye is letting go, and it means we have to acknowledge that we are all changing and moving on. Nothing lasts forever.

In our youth, perhaps we celebrated that nothing lasts forever. Commonly, as we grow old, we long for sameness. Let's help each other remember the comfort of change. Our journey is about change. That's why we're here.

I will watch my life closely today. It will not be the same tomorrow. This journey moves me along moment by moment.

—from *Keepers of the Wisdom*

July 28

Other people's perspectives are valid.

Many of us have believed our opinions on all matters are right. This has put us at odds with family, friends, and strangers. Accepting that every person's perspective is valid, at least for that person, may seem out of the question at first. But after growing accustomed to the idea, we will find great relief, knowing that we don't have to be in conflict anymore. We are so much freer when we respect others' opinions.

The best way to remember that others have valid perspectives is by developing the habit of momentarily pausing before responding to another's words or actions. We will get good at letting others "be." And *we* will feel so much better for it.

I will momentarily pause before responding to others today. This will save me from lots of tension.

—from *A Life of My Own*

July 29

Woman must not accept; she must challenge. She must not be awed by that which has been built up around her; she must reverence that woman in her which struggles for expression.

—MARGARET SANGER

Our desire to grow, to make a place for ourselves in the world of our friends, to know that we have counted in the lives of others, is healthy and necessary to our existence as whole women. The inner urging to move ahead, to try a new approach to an old problem, to go after a new job, to learn a new skill, is evidence of God's eternal Spirit within.

Our meaning in this life is found through following the guidance that beckons us toward these new horizons, perhaps new friends, even new locations. We can trust the urge. We can reverence the urge. It will not lead us astray, provided we do not try to lead it. We each have a special gift to express in this life among those to whom we've been led.

For years, many of us quelled the inner urge out of fear; but, fortunately, it didn't desert us. To be human is to have a constant desire to be more than we are. The fears still come, but as we move through them, with the support of other women, other friends, the program gives us the thrill of achievement. We know there is meaning in our existence.

The need to grow, to change, to affect the world around us is part of God's plan for each of us. I will trust the urge; I will let it guide my steps.

—from *Each Day a New Beginning*

July 30

Patience is bitter, but its fruit is sweet.
—LIDA CLARKSON

We all want life to unfold according to our plan. After all, we are certain we know what's best for us. But hindsight quickly reminds us that few, if any, of us had included recovery in a Twelve Step program as part of our life's plan. Yet here we are, and we are now more content than we've ever been in our lives. How did this happen?

We have come to accept that God has worked in our lives in spite of ourselves. We have been protected and guided all along the way, even though on occasion we stubbornly attempted to force open doors that were not beneficial to our growth. Fortunately our Higher Power never gave up on us. We will fulfill our purpose with all the help we need when the time is right.

Remembering that opportunities come to us when their time is right allows us to wait and trust.

My patience will pay off today. I can be certain that what comes to me today is on time.

—from *A Woman's Spirit*

July 31

Seek peacefulness, not specific answers.

Because we think we need to know exactly how to proceed in all areas of life and because we harbor particular wants and desires, we seek complicated, detailed solutions for every situation that surfaces. We muddle our minds with worry over how we should do our part in whatever circumstance beckons. Considering the strength of the ordinary ego, that's not surprising. The ego wants what it wants when it wants it!

There is another way to do our part, however. We can dispense with the idea of detail all together. That may seem unusual but only because we are so accustomed to letting the ego run our lives. Seeking no answer, no solution can be refreshing. Desiring peace rather than a complicated agenda of activities is so much less burdensome. We'll feel like new people, as if a miracle has occurred. And indeed it has. Changing our minds about what to seek changes everything about what we get.

What I seek, I will find. I will quietly remember this today.

—from *Daily Meditations for Practicing the* Course

August

August 1

Don't just want. Choose.
—PATRICIA BENSON

For many of us the fog is only beginning to clear. It takes awhile to understand that all along life has been about making choices. Because we were under the influence, we inadvertently rolled into many situations with unclear intentions. Not being conscious of our choices, however, doesn't absolve us of the responsibility for making them. Now we have the opportunity, with the help of the program, to take charge of our choices. We can, with thought, make responsible choices.

We are assured the gift of empowerment when we actively take charge of our choices. We used to want things to work out without doing our part or asking for what we needed. Or we never consciously made choices. What has become so very clear is that not choosing is in fact choosing! And, no doubt, we are still saddled with the results of some of the "choices" we never intended to make. No longer does this need to be our life pattern. Today is a new day, and this program is giving us every tool we need to embark on a new course.

I will grow in confidence the more I consciously choose among my many options today.

—from *A Woman's Spirit*

August 2

Each day is different and has a surprise in it, like a Cracker Jack box.

—ALPHA ENGLISH

It's interesting to ponder the notion of surprise. Not every one of them, in old age, is all that welcome. Hearing bad news about a friend or having a special trip we'd been counting on canceled can leave us dismayed and worried, right along with surprised. Seeking solace from others while cultivating a willingness to accept that all things happen for a reason gives us the armor we need to make the best of every situation and disappointment.

It's an interesting image to think of each day as a box of Cracker Jacks. The moments of our lives have been very tasty. Some were sweet, some were a bit salty, and there were always wholly unexpected moments, the surprises that we were ready for even though we may not have imagined as much. We can look forward to the same daily agenda throughout the remaining years.

Does it help to know that there is a divine plan unfolding in our lives? Many of us find comfort in that. All of us can cultivate that belief.

I am ready for my surprise today! It is meant for me at this time.

—from *Keepers of the Wisdom*

August 3

The change of one simple behavior can affect other behaviors and thus change many things.

—JEAN BAER

Our behavior tells others and ourselves who we are. Frequently, we find ourselves behaving in ways that keep us stuck or embarrass us. Or we may feel deep shame for our behavior in a certain instance. Our behavior will never totally please us. But deciding we want to change some behavior and using the program to help us is a first step.

Remember, imperfections are human and very acceptable. However, changing a particular behavior, maybe deciding to take a walk every morning rather than sleeping 30 extra minutes, will change how we feel about ourselves. And a minor change such as this can have a remarkable effect on our outlook, our attitudes.

The dilemma for many of us for so long was the fear we couldn't change. But we can. And we can help each other change, too.

One small change today—a smile at the first person I meet—meditation before dinner—a few minutes of exercise—will help me chart a new course. I will encourage another woman to join me in this effort too, and I will be on my way.

—from *Each Day a New Beginning*

August 4

The outer world mirrors our inner thoughts in every instance.

We make whatever we see, plain and simple! If we're not happy, the responsibility lies with us to make something else, and we can do this in an instant by changing our thoughts.

As novices to the *Course,* we may find it difficult to change our minds. A tiny bit of practice, on the other hand, reveals how easy it is. So what if we have to keep "changing our minds." Every time we replace a negative thought with one of love or peace, we'll feel relief. We'll also feel empowered and hopeful in every situation we encounter.

It's not easy to understand how thought projection works. Perhaps we don't have to. But believing in the principle and then thinking only love demonstrates how what we think reflects back to us. How we see others changes forever when we embrace this principle.

Reflecting on love and God today will emphatically change my experience.

—from *Daily Meditations for Practicing the* Course

August 5

When doors are locked, look for the key.

For most of our lives, we have pushed or been pushed to persevere, to never give up trying to attain worthy goals. Thus learning now that we need to surrender to God's will seems counter to all that had helped us succeed in years past.

What we come to understand is that we need not give up our goals; indeed, we should strive to accomplish them. But when we find doors closing in our faces or get repeated rejections for our efforts, we need to look to our Higher Power for understanding. Perhaps our direction is not consistent with God's will. Surrendering, then, becomes the solution. And the right goal for us will emerge. Getting on track with God will assure us peaceful well-being.

Am I in tune with God's plan for me today?

—from *A Life of My Own*

August 6

I got a lot of my value system from the books I read
as a child.

—RUTH CASEY

Our value systems were honed from a number of sources.
Parents, peers, teachers, the church all made significant
contributions. But so did all the experiences we had. Everything we did or read or discussed with others had an impact on how our values were formed.

Having a set of values to guide us has been extremely
important to how our lives have evolved. We struggled far
less with decision making when we knew who we were.
Our lives continue to be fraught with the occasional
struggle. How fortunate that we have the experience of
seeking the inner guidance we need in any circumstance.
Our value systems are safely tucked away there.

Getting old sets up many obstacles; we don't need any
extra ones. If we are uncertain of how to behave in particular situations, we complicate our lives. If we find ourselves
in this predicament on occasion, perhaps it's because we
have not sought the wisdom within. It has not departed
us. Our values never leave; it's just our use of them that
may get rusty.

My values will guide me in handling any problems today.

—from *Keepers of the Wisdom*

August 7

Who is making our decisions?

Nothing external to us has any meaning except what we bring to it. Therefore, if a problem arises, we have to look solely at ourselves. The advantage is we need look only to ourselves if we want to change our lives. Playing the waiting game, as many of us have done—waiting for people to change, waiting for circumstances to change, waiting for expectations to change—need not detain us any longer. If we want anything to be different, let's get moving!

Making changes is not complicated, unless it's another person we want to change. That's an impossibility. However, we will discover how changed they will seem when we make a change in ourselves. Whatever we see in others depends on how we look at them, and which *inner eye* we look through. This principle is set.

Who we put in charge of how we see today will determine everything: the situations that arise, the actions we take, and the decisions we make. It's a monumental choice.

I will be thoughtful about my choices today. If I want a good day, I'll rely on the Holy Spirit.

—from *Daily Meditations for Practicing the* Course

August 8

*If you are truly calm, you stand a chance of
surviving much, but calmness is intermittent
with me.*

—FLORIDA SCOTT-MAXWELL

The calm we feel is proportionate to the faith we have in
a Higher Power. Some days are calmer than others. Why
does our faith waver?

We too easily dispense with the daily routines that can
help us be at peace: spending a few moments alone, reading some words of wisdom, praying to our Higher Power
for care and guidance. We have probably heard someone
say, "If you feel far away from God, it's not because God
moved." Is it our habit to rely on God for every solution?
Do we believe that every experience can benefit us as long
as we acknowledge God in it? Do we make it a practice to
include God in every decision we make or action we take?
When we can answer yes to all of these questions, we'll discover that our faith no longer wavers. We'll know that God
is close and calm is upon us.

*I am calm in the company of my Higher Power. Today will run
smoothly.*

—from *A Woman's Spirit*

August 9

We can change our minds, nothing more.

Nothing can disturb us if we realize we only need to change our minds about it. No person can get under our skin, no situation can haunt or frighten us, no longer would the anticipation of a future event hold us hostage. The freedom suggested here isn't imaginary. It's the very miracle that adopting the *Course* principles guarantees.

We have all spent countless years trying to change other people and the circumstances in our lives. We've done this because of our own fears of not fitting in. If only someone or something else were different, we'd be safe, we thought. Our fears only grew. The number of situations that we tried to control unsuccessfully only multiplied. At long last we have discovered a new approach to living.

How do we change our minds? We ask this tiny question of the Holy Spirit: "Will you help me see what's happening now in another way?" Our minds will change instantly. We may have to repeat the request, many times at first, but we will get results.

I can have a different vision of everything I see today if the one I've made up doesn't bring me peace.

—from *Daily Meditations for Practicing the* Course

August 10

It only takes one person to change your life—you.
—RUTH CASEY

Change is not easy, but it's absolutely unavoidable. Doors will close. Barriers will surface. Frustrations will mount. Nothing stays the same forever, and it's such folly to wish otherwise. Growth accompanies positive change; determining to risk the outcome resulting from a changed behavior or attitude will enhance our self-perceptions. We will have moved forward; in every instance our lives will be influenced by making a change that only each of us can make.

We have all dreaded the changes we knew we had to make. Perhaps even now we fear some impending changes. Where might they take us? It's difficult accepting that the outcome is not ours to control. Only the effort is ours. The solace is that positive changes, which we know are right for us and other people in our lives, are never going to take us astray. In fact, they are necessary for the smooth path just beyond this stumbling block.

When we are troubled by circumstances in our lives, a change is called for, a change that we must initiate. When we reflect on our recent as well as distant past, we will remember that the changes we most dreaded again and again have positively influenced our lives in untold ways.

Change ushers in glad, not bad, tidings.

—from *Each Day a New Beginning*

August 11

We need to give back, to plow something back in the ground.

—JIM BURNS

It's not uncommon to hear an acquaintance say, "I want to give back." But are we convinced of just how important that is? What does "giving back" really mean? There are many answers. It's about staying involved with the human community, even when we don't have to. It's about choosing the stimulation of others' ideas over the loneliness of self-absorption. It's about offering our wisdom to those who can profit from it.

We are here by design. What we have learned, accomplished, and shared with others were parts of our "assignment." And the proof that we aren't *done yet* is that we're still here. There must be additional lessons for us to learn. The men and women who accompany us on our journey today need us for their lessons, too.

It's comforting to know that we don't have to discern the particulars of what to give back, what to still accomplish, what to yet learn from our experiences. If we are open and trust our inner spirit, we'll do the right thing, whatever that is at this stage of our lives.

Today I will be alert to invitations to join with others on our mutual journey.

—from *Keepers of the Wisdom*

August 12

The alcoholic isn't the problem.

We come into the program certain that we'd be happy if only the alcoholic would quit drinking. Surprisingly, he or she often does, and then we discover we're still unhappy. Our problem isn't the alcoholic. While it might be true that living with an alcoholic can be stressful and his or her behavior can complicate our plans, *we* decided to give up our happiness. The alcoholic never took it from us.

Meeting with other people who are content, even joyful, in spite of sharing their lives with an active alcoholic gives us valuable food for thought. Happiness is a by-product of how we live our lives, not how others live theirs. Giving the drinker or the boss or the noisy neighbor power over how we feel is always an option, but the payoff is not what we really want.

We want to be happy. We deserve to be happy. We can be happy if that's what we make up our minds to be.

My unhappiness can't be blamed on someone else. Immaturity makes me want to blame others, but my program friends won't let me get away with it. Today I will choose to be happy.

—from *A Life of My Own*

August 13

Nothing has to change.

So many times a day we lament a particular situation, certain that our lives could be vastly improved if only it changed. And when that doesn't seem possible, we focus on the people involved, in hopes that they will change. Can it be true that nothing has to change in order for our experience to be different? Indeed, that's the case. But how?

When the particulars of a situation stay the same, it's natural for us to assume that our reaction and the outcome will be the same too. That's what past experience has taught us. But we are learning something different now, and it's vastly important. It can change every experience we'll ever have; consequently, our lives will unfold in a way that's unimaginable to us now.

We are learning that we can see any experience in a wholly unexpected way simply by seeking another perspective. Not a single aspect has to change for us to see it differently. That's miraculous! Our lives will never be the same.

I can handle whatever is happening today. How I see it is in my control.

—from *Daily Meditations for Practicing the* Course

August 14

I've got a long list of things to talk to God about.
—FRAN COYNE

What we expect about the afterlife contributes to our level of comfort in this life. If death scares us, if we think punishment awaits us for our every transgression, we'll live in constant dread of the inevitable. This, in turn, will influence how we experience all the situations we still have to live through. Fear becomes all-encompassing, and it distorts every detail of our perception. Living without fear has just as measurable an impact.

The final stage of life can be seen as an opportunity to seek answers to the situations that have troubled us over the years; this can redefine how we think about death. It lends an air of excitement about the final phase. It also reflects a far different understanding about God, God's role, and our part in the *divine* plan. To have a discussion with God, as Fran suggests, implies one considers God a friend, a confidant—surely not someone ready to inflict grave harm on us.

Being able to seek an explanation for all the mysteries of our lives and the lives of our loved ones gives death a significantly different feel. It can become an experience that we anticipate almost eagerly. Is that so bad?

There are experiences in my life that I never understood. I can now bring these unresolved concerns to God.

—from *Keepers of the Wisdom*

August 15

❧

Feelings are triggered by thoughts.

How quick we are to blame someone else for our anger or our hurt feelings. Blaming other people is easy. What's hard is accepting that our thoughts cause our feelings. Our program friends will help us see that taking responsibility for our thoughts and feelings empowers us to change our lives in dramatic ways. And none of us came into this program content with our life.

It may seem grandiose to think we can change our lives. But we can. We can change the content of our minds, which in turn changes the feelings we harbor. We choose how to see a situation. We choose how we react to a set of circumstances. We are in charge. Being happy is a choice.

I can't blame anyone else for how I feel today. My thoughts are in charge of that.

—from *A Life of My Own*

August 16

Every human being has, like Socrates, an attendant spirit; and wise are they who obey its signals. If it does not always tell us what to do, it always cautions us what not to do.

—LYDIA M. CHILD

Our Spirit is our inner guide. And our Spirit never, never, gives us wrong directions. Because we're human, it's all too easy to deny the voice from within. Some call it conscience. And our behavior, maybe frequently, maybe occasionally, belies what our conscience knows is right. We suffer for it.

We are trying to be healthy—emotionally, spiritually, physically. Each day we can make progress. With each action we take, we have a choice. Our Spirit, our conscience, should be consulted. Right choices make for right actions that will emotionally and spiritually benefit us and the other persons close to us.

It's comforting to rely on the inner voice. It assures us we're never alone. No decision has to be made alone. No wrong action need ever be taken. A sense of security accompanies the partnership between each of us and our Spirit.

I will let the partnership work for me today.

—from *Each Day a New Beginning*

August 17

God's will never takes me where his grace will not
sustain me.

—RUTH HUMLECKER

Letting go of our own will in favor of fulfilling God's is certainly in our best interests. However, it is not always easy to
do. We often cling tenaciously to a dream gone sour or a
relationship long since dead because of our fear of the
unknown. Although a good lesson comes from our past
lives—we clearly see that God's plan would have been better for us than our own—perhaps the best lesson comes
from our recovering lives today. We didn't get here all by
ourselves, and God didn't help us find this program only
to abandon us. We are in God's care now and always.

Believing that we will survive every experience, no matter how inadequate or frightened we feel, will come as we
develop trust. Acting as if we believe that God is in charge
will carry us until the belief becomes solid faith. And it
will. We have been promised that. God's grace will see to it.

*I will trust my life to God today. Again and again I will turn my
life over and believe that all is well.*

—from *A Woman's Spirit*

August 18

We can't hear God's voice when we're judging someone.

We don't always want to hear God's voice. There are moments when we love the power we feel while judging others.
The high is short-lived, however. Inevitably we experience
guilt commensurate with our judgments.

Fortunately, God's voice of love and forgiveness quietly
waits for our willingness to hear it. We'll not see our experiences or our companions in the same way when we listen
to God's message regarding them. Why would we ever
choose to turn away?

The answer lies in the insanity of the ego. If we're not
extremely cautious in our focus, it will grab our attention
and command our reactions. We can think only attack
when the ego is in charge. One or the other voice will always be heard. Which do we want it to be?

Today I will remember that judging others jeopardizes my sense of peace.

—from *Daily Meditations for Practicing the* Course

August 19

*I hope I won't get so I can't walk, but if I do, I'll be
grateful that I can still move. People who can move
have so much to be grateful for.*

—ALPHA ENGLISH

If more of us were as determined as Alpha to take responsibility for making our lives better, far fewer of us would
be harboring anger, depression, or waning confidence. We
can all be certain that as we age, our levels of agility and
energy will decline, but that doesn't mean we can't still go
where we want. It merely means we may have to make an
alternate plan for how we get there.

Let's never assume our lives have to change totally. Giving up our dreams, regardless of their nature, may be far
more injurious to us than proceeding with even risky
undertakings. Getting old doesn't mean giving up. We all
know individuals who settled for that, however. And many
of them appear to be waiting for their end. What sepa-
rates us from them? Attitude. A simple change of mind
makes all the difference in who we are and who we can yet
become.

Let's never forget that doing the "next best thing" will
always bring us contentment.

*I will have many opportunities to move forward or sit still today.
God, please help me choose the next best thing.*

—from Keepers of the Wisdom

August 20

*Looking for good in other people improves
our attitude.*

We weren't born critical and negative. We developed those
behaviors. And for many of us they became habit. They
also became self-defeating. If we saw only the faults and
not the assets in others, we probably assumed they saw the
same in us. We were all losers in the process.

We have come to the program because we are tired of
losing! We want to feel better about ourselves; one of the
easiest ways to accomplish this is to feel better about others. It's really not so difficult to see the better side of others. Initially it's a decision. Then it's willingness to practice
the behavior. The hardest part is bringing our minds back
to the positive when they wander through their old stomp-
ing grounds.

Asking God for help will begin the process of change
for us. Not dismissing even the smallest positive quality in
another will improve our perspective.

I will see only the good in my friends today. Practice will help.

—from *A Life of My Own*

August 21

We tend to think of the rational as a higher order,
but it is the emotional that marks our lives. One
often learns more from ten days of agony than from
ten years of contentment.

—MERLE SHAIN

Pain stretches us. It pushes us toward others. It encourages us to pray. It invites us to rely on many resources, particularly those within.

We develop our character while handling painful times. Pain offers wisdom. It prepares us to help other women whose experiences repeat our own. Our own pain offers us the stories that help another who is lost and needs our guidance.

When we reflect on our past for a moment, we can recall the pain we felt last month or last year; the pain of a lost love, or the pain of no job and many bills; perhaps the pain of children leaving home, or the death of a near and dear friend. It might have seemed to us that we couldn't cope. But we did, somehow, and it felt good. Coping strengthened us.

What we forget, even now, is that we need never experience a painful time alone. The agony that accompanies a wrenching situation is dissipated as quickly and as silently as the entrance of our higher power, when called upon.

I long for contentment. And I deserve those times. But without life's pain I would fail to recognize the value of contentment.

—from Each Day a New Beginning

August 22

~⊃

You're right where you're supposed to be.
—ANONYMOUS

Few circumstances in our lives evolve perfectly. Health problems develop, jobs don't work out, or, even worse, significant others leave us. For a time we can't cope. We become angry, distraught, or full of self-pity. When a sponsor or friend says "You're just where you need to be," we want to scream. With time, however, we usually calm down and accept this message.

A divine plan is unfolding in our lives. We don't know ahead of time the route we will take or the destination we will arrive at. Our wisdom is simply the certainty that we are "in the right place at the right time." Our Higher Power is in charge, and whatever our experiences, they are preparing us for the rest of our journey.

I am where I need to be today. And God is planning my trip.

—from *A Woman's Spirit*

August 23

Destructive relationships can be transformed.

Friends generally recommend that we get out of destructive relationships. That may be good advice. However, there is another idea to consider. We might choose to redefine the relationship, but it takes our genuine willingness to change how we perceive the relationship now. And if it's physically or mentally destructive, we may not choose to do that. Indeed, perhaps we shouldn't.

The important idea here is that we can create a shift in our perception of a relationship. We can't do it alone, and we can't do it with the ego's help. We can do it, however, if we invite the Holy Spirit into the relationship. It helps when both people want the Holy Spirit's involvement, but even if only one requests it, a change in how he or she perceives the relationship will occur.

One might still choose to leave it, but the reasons for doing so will be different. It won't be done in anger or fear. It will happen because it should happen; the guidance was offered and accepted. The destruction has ended and this relationship has been transformed.

My relationships can be changed today. If I want one to be different, I simply need to seek help from the Holy Spirit.

—from *Daily Meditations for Practicing the* Course

August 24

In my many years as a teacher, I tried to impart to children to "do unto others as you would have them do unto you."

—EVA WINES

Passing on wisdom such as this is invaluable. If only one of Eva's students chose to live accordingly, the world was made a better place; Eva's example was powerful. Even as her health was failing, she lived according to her own dictates. In her gentle presence, one felt her peacefulness, and feeling peace from any source is all many of us need to be prepared to pass it on.

Because our lives have changed, because we are out of the main work force, because we have far fewer responsibilities, we sometimes think we aren't needed anymore. It's quite possibly true that we aren't needed for the activities that demanded our attention in the previous decades. But *our work* isn't done. These times we live in might suggest to some of us that our most important work lies ahead, in fact.

Conveying the feeling of peace to someone else, be it stranger or friend, is doing exceedingly important work. For much of our lives we might not have known just what we "taught" others. But we can all know now how it feels to express love and the gift of peace to another. The legacy we can leave behind will make a difference in the world. Let's do our part.

I need do so little today to make a difference. Sharing my peace with someone else will do it.

—from *Keepers of the Wisdom*

August 25

*The most important legacy I've passed on to
my children is loyalty to one another and the
willingness to help someone else.*

—HELEN CASEY

How we behave toward others always serves as an example
to all who observe us. No doubt some of us wish we'd given
more thought to the example we set for our children and
friends. Let's not be too hard on ourselves, though. What's
past is past. Communicating with our loved ones about
our earlier shortcomings gives us freedom from them. It
also offers us another opportunity for example-setting.

Valuing loyalty reveals so much about the spirit that
abides in Helen. The first thing it says is that the Spirit in
someone else has been valued too, by her. And is there any
more important expression than this? That she can see the
results in the lives of her children blesses her now, in the
same way that her example has blessed them throughout
their lives.

Life's lessons are so subtly passed on. Often we're not
even aware of our roles as teachers. However, observation
of those who grew up closest to us reveals just what we
taught. There's still time to alter the legacy if we have
changed our minds about what's important.

*I will serve as someone's teacher today. That's how life works.
Someone else will show me their way of seeing too.*

—from *Keepers of the Wisdom*

August 26

"What we hear here, stays here."

Each of us who comes to a Twelve Step meeting harbors at least a tiny fear, initially, about the safety of sharing secrets that have kept us stuck. Some of us have haunting memories of earlier times when our disclosures weren't kept in confidence. Today, however, as we listen to the openness and honesty of other people, we are assured that this is a safe place—to be and to share.

Having a place we can go to unburden ourselves begins the healing process, perhaps even before we have begun to share. Just knowing we can talk freely as soon as we are ready, that we have friends who want to listen and help, diminishes the seduction of isolation. And that's where we have lived for a long time.

Keeping the secrets divulged by friends in a meeting creates a bond, one that is strengthened with each disclosure. For many of us, this is the first time in our lives we have felt needed, listened to, and equal to the people around us. What a blessing this program is!

I will keep all my conversations confidential today. I want others to trust me just as I want to trust them.

—from *A Life of My Own*

August 27

There is a Divine plan for our lives.

While in the midst of turmoil, we sometimes forget that our Higher Power is available to ease the pain. We need to remember that whatever we experience is for our growth and is part of God's plan that is unfolding in our lives, a plan that feels painful simply because we forget that God is the architect.

Taking time every day to reflect on the past and the changes we've survived will help us acknowledge that a plan has been unfolding. Most of us are in a safer, better spot now than ever before. The myriad worries have been resolved. We have the support of genuine, loving friends. No experience, no matter how trying, has to be handled alone. And this is all part of God's plan.

I will eagerly remember that God is orchestrating my life today. Every experience is part of the Divine plan.

—from *A Life of My Own*

August 28

❧

...suffering... no matter how multiplied... is always individual.

—ANNE MORROW LINDBERGH

Knowing that others have survived experiences equally devastating gives us hope, but it doesn't diminish our own personal suffering. Nor should it; out of suffering comes new understanding. Suffering also encourages our appreciation of the lighter, easier times. Pain experienced fully enhances the times of pleasure.

Our sufferings are singular, individual, and lonely. But our experiences with it can be shared, thereby lessening the power they have over us. Sharing our pain with another woman also helps her remember that her pain, too, is survivable.

Suffering softens us, helps us to feel more compassion and love toward another. Our sense of belonging to the human race, our recognition of the interdependence and kinship of us all, are the most cherished results of the gift of pain.

Each of our sufferings, sharing them as we do, strengthens me and heals my wounds of alienation.

—from *Each Day a New Beginning*

August 29

Asking God for help has finally become a part of my life. Now I'm learning to quiet myself to hear God's response.

—JOAN ROHDE

No problem is too insignificant for us to look to God for guidance. And every problem gives us an opportunity to strengthen our spiritual development. As we rely more on God for our sense of direction, we will encounter fewer situations that cause us turmoil. Trusting God's presence and guidance lessens the confusion that in past years may have crippled us.

Most of us came into this program with little or no belief in a loving Higher Power. It may have taken frequent suggestions from sponsors and other people in recovery for us to be willing to ask for the help we were promised. But finally we cleared that hurdle. Immediately we faced another one. Asking for help, we found, was the easier part; listening for God's reply was harder.

But the right reply will come to us at the right time. We will sense the answer we're looking for when the time for knowing it is right.

I will include my Higher Power in all my problem solving today. The solution I need will be mine if I patiently wait for the response.

—from A Woman's Spirit

August 30

Every thought we hold manifests somewhere.

Consider this: If we choose to think of a co-worker as detrimental to our success at work, we'll respond to him in a suspicious, attacking manner. He'll likely respond in kind. We'll have created a situation that mirrors our perception. Every thought we hold manifests somewhere. This extremely powerful idea is both frightening and exhilarating.

If the principle works this successfully for negative thinking, can we expect it to work similarly when we hold only love in our minds? That's the good news. Whatever we hold in our minds, whichever *voice* forms our thoughts, determines how we see our companions and how we experience our lives minute by minute. In other words, if we are having a bad day, we are having "bad" thoughts. The decision to change our minds, thus our thoughts, can be made as often as necessary.

I will be accountable for how my day is going. If I don't like how it feels, it's up to me to monitor my thoughts and change them.

—from *Daily Meditations for Practicing the* Course

August 31

Everything has its wonders, even darkness and
silence, and I learn, whatever state I may be in,
therein to be content.

—HELEN KELLER

There is wonder in the moment, if we but look for it, let it
touch us, believe in it. And with the recognition and cele-
bration of the wonder comes the joy we desire and await.

Being wholly in tune with the present moment is how
we'll come to know the spiritual essence that connects all
of life. We search for peace, happiness, and contentment
outside of ourselves. We need instead to discover it within
us, now and always, in whatever we are experiencing.

We can let our experiences wash over us. Longing for a
different time, a distant place, a new situation breeds discontent. It prevents us from the thrill, the gifts offered in
this present moment. But they are there.

We can practice feeling joyful in the present, be thrilled
with the realization that right now, all is well. All is always
well. Life is full of mystery and wonder and each moment
of our awareness adds to the wonder.

*I am moving forward; we all are. I am on target. I am participat-
ing in a glorious, wonderful drama. Let me jump for joy. I have
been specially blessed.*

—from Each Day a New Beginning

September

September 1

*I have to remember to tell the negative committee
that meets in my head to sit down and shut up.*
—KATHY KENDALL

Why does it seem easier to get trapped in negative thinking than it does to have positive expectations? Maybe it's
only a matter of habit. We may be proficient at expecting
the worst outcomes, but with the support and the example
of friends who share our journey today, we can break that
habit. And we'll discover that it's not that difficult.

Let's begin by making small attempts. In the past our
mind seemed to fill up with random thoughts, as if it were
a newsreel produced by an outsider. Today, as quick as a
blink, we can fast-forward the picture to one we prefer. We
can be the full-time "producer" of our own newsreel. That's
the good news!

Our thoughts and attitudes are there by our choice. We
must acknowledge that. We can neither blame nor give
credit to anyone but ourselves. We can make a habit of
positive thinking. Let's begin right now.

*I will focus on positive thoughts today. Remembering that my
thoughts are of my own making, every time, makes it easier to
switch channels.*

—from *A Woman's Spirit*

September 2

Life is so much easier if you ride the horse in the direction it's going.

—ANONYMOUS

There is a pattern to our lives. Our Higher Power has always wanted the best for us. Had we trusted the natural flow of our experiences instead of trying to control people and outcomes, we'd have experienced less pain and lots more joy. It's not that life won't have difficult lessons to teach us on occasion. It will and they may hurt. But we must remember that God will never give us what we can't handle and, furthermore, that we'll have the guidance we need to meet our challenges.

Going against our inner urges never gives us peace. The wisdom that resides within is a gift from our Higher Power. Let's never forget that.

I will be peaceful today if I follow the voice of my heart.

—from *A Woman's Spirit*

September 3

~○

The absence of love is fear.

Fear haunts many of us. Fear of what the alcoholic in our lives is doing, fear of what the neighbors think, fear of losing our job, fear of being abandoned—the list is endless. It's the lack of connection to a Higher Power that invites the fear in. Yet when we feel God's presence, we can bask in the warmth of love, giving it and receiving it. And fear is gone.

Admittedly, we don't always feel God's presence, even when we ask "for knowledge of God's will." But a tool this program has given us—acting as if—can help. When we act as if we feel love for our companions and co-workers, we begin to feel at peace, connected to God, and the fear dissipates. The wonderful realization is that we don't have to feel God's presence first to be loving; we can get to God through having faith that His love will replace our fears.

I will shed any fears I have today by making the effort to love the people around me. My Higher Power will be close too.

—from *A Life of My Own*

September 4

Self-control is one of the greatest skills I've learned.
—JIM BURNS

Most of us assume we have mastered self-control by now. And perhaps we have. A good test is to monitor how we respond to a nagging spouse or a disrespectful postman or vile-mouthed teenager. Do instances such as these make us angry or resentful? If so, we aren't exerting adequate self-control. Letting another's behavior, no matter how petty, disturb our inner peace means we aren't in control of ourselves. But we can be. There is still time to learn how, and most of us have all the time we need.

Why is self-control so valuable? Getting agitated feels good sometimes. We may think it's superior to boredom. But in truth, losing control of our emotions means we are always in the control of someone else. That too often means we are on a roller-coaster of ups and downs that exhaust us. Illness can even result. Another benefit of self-control is that we can lessen the turmoil around us, rather than add to it. As we have discussed before, the impact of any action or thought or quiet response is never ending. It's quite analogous to the pebble skipped across the pond. We are making subtle contributions to the world around us whether we are conscious of it or not. Let's be more careful of our input.

I will consider my input in all situations carefully today. What someone else does need not determine my actions.

—from *Keepers of the Wisdom*

September 5

❧

Changing one thing at a time is quite enough.

There are times when we feel overwhelmed by our short-comings. And it seems that most of our friends have few, if any. Of course, that too is one of our shortcomings: We compare ourselves with other people and never quite measure up.

We each are a collection of assets and shortcomings. That's the human condition. But we can strengthen the traits we like and de-emphasize the rest. We just can't do it all at once.

First, we choose one element of our behavior, either an asset or a defect. Then we decide what we want to do with it today. There is a perfect formula for making changes in our lives. Keeping our focus small and our expectations reasonable allow us to experience the success we deserve. Little by little, applying this formula regularly, we will become the people we envision ourselves to be.

I am much more than whatever shortcoming caused me pain yesterday. Today is a new day, and I can help one of my assets blossom by demonstrating it repeatedly.

—from *A Life of My Own*

September 6

To oppose something is to maintain it.
—URSULA K. LE GUIN

Most of our struggles are with other persons or perhaps situations we want to change. We discover that our continual opposition adds fuel to the fires (at least our own internal ones). But can we turn our backs when we feel justified in our opposition? There's perhaps no more difficult action to take than to walk away from those situations we feel so strongly about, but the wisdom of this program says, "Let go and let God." And when we do let go, as if by magic, relief comes. The fires die out. That which we opposed is less troubling, maybe even gone. We no longer feel the need to struggle today. The need may rise again, but again we can turn to our higher power. Trusting that relief awaits us, ensures its arrival.

As women we rediscover many opportunities for opposition, too many persons and situations that make our changing roles difficult—too many persons who don't easily accept our changing characters. We must share with one another the strength to let go and let God.

I maintain my struggles with righteous behavior. They lose their sting when they lose my opposition. I will step aside and let God.

—from *Each Day a New Beginning*

September 7

Most of us were on our way to an awful destination, and it's doubtful that we realized it at the time. In fact, we probably were satisfied with the direction we'd headed in and fiercely fought the forces that moved us off our chosen path. Fortunately, we lost the battle. In the process we gained this life, but it has taken time for us to understand how lucky we are to have been "saved."

God's grace has blessed us. We can call it "luck" or "karma" or "good planning" or an "accident," but we hear those in recovery calling it grace. We know that they are right. Something intervened and changed the course of our lives.

We may not yet know just what our new direction is, but we can be certain that if we listen to the still, small voice within, we'll understand the meaning of the grace that's been bestowed on us.

My future is special. Today I'll be shown what I need to know for living the next twenty-four hours.

—from *A Woman's Spirit*

September 8

What can I learn from this situation?

Everything that happens to us can be spiritually enlightening. Trusting this principle can lessen the trauma of any situation. The loss of a loved one hurts, but we remember that God never leaves us. The disappearance of a favorite possession may upset us, but we know possessions don't love us and we can survive without them.

We're moving along a learning curve, passing other students one day and being passed the next. Our destination is the same; we're going home to rejoin God and forget this tiny, mad nightmare we have been living.

We find great relief in remembering that no experience is so big or so awful we can't quickly decipher the lesson and move on. Not getting bogged down in trivia refreshes us.

Today's lessons have my name on them.

—from *Daily Meditations for Practicing the* Course

September 9

I like to think my purpose in life is to love.
—JANE NAKKEN

Most would agree that we are *here* for a reason. Reflecting on where we have come from and the changes that have occurred in our lives, we are convinced that some Power has been present every step of the way. We do have both a purpose and a protector.

The panic to determine our specific purpose is not unusual for addicts like us. We demand absolutes; guesswork frightens us. But finding a sponsor who will tell us that our purpose doesn't matter will be to our benefit. From her we'll learn to take our experiences in stride, trusting that we'll discover who we are and what we need to do next if we accept life as it unfolds.

If we must have a purpose now, choosing to believe our purpose is loving others eases our way. And really, there is no purpose more worthy anyway.

Today I will express to others the love I know my Higher Power has for me. It's the best action I can take.

—from *A Woman's Spirit*

September 10

In the face of an obstacle which is impossible to
overcome, stubbornness is stupid.

—SIMONE DE BEAUVOIR

Sudden obstacles, barriers in the way of our progress,
doors that unexpectedly close, may confuse, frustrate, even
depress us. The knowledge that we seldom understand
just what is best for us comes slowly. And we generally
fight it, even after we've begun to understand. Fortunately,
the better path will keep drawing us to it.

We may wonder why a door seems to have closed. Our
paths are confounded only when our steps have gone
astray. Doors do not close unless a new direction is called
for. We must learn to trust that no obstacle is without its
purpose, however baffling it may seem.

The program can help us understand the unexpected.
We perhaps need to focus on the first three Steps when an
obstacle has surfaced. We may need to accept powerlessness, believe there is a higher power in control, and look to
it for guidance. We may also need to remind ourselves that
fighting an obstacle, pushing against a closed door, will
only heighten our frustration. *Acceptance of what is* will
open our minds and our hearts to the better road to travel
at this time.

*The obstacles confronting me invite me to grow, to move beyond
my present self. They offer me chances to be the woman I always
dreamed of being. I will be courageous. I am not alone.*

—from *Each Day a New Beginning*

September 11

ᕗ

But for the grace of God . . .

Sometimes we were smug and passed judgment on other people, certain that we'd never be in their circumstances. However, most of us never thought we'd be in our current circumstances either. We simply can't know what the future holds for us, and if we did we'd probably be terrified, certain we couldn't handle whatever burdens we might have to bear.

It's no accident that we're in a Twelve Step program. We couldn't have imagined this as a necessary part of our lives a few years ago, but it is, and our lives have begun to feel purposeful and guided. Developing trust that a Higher Power has always been in charge gives us confidence that we'll not be led into waters so troubling that we can't wade through them.

Our lives feel so much freer now. Remembering that God's grace has brought us to this point can relieve us of the compulsion to worry about the future.

My Higher Power has saved me thus far. I am confident that I will be protected today too.

—from *A Life of My Own*

September 12

People who love animals generally love people, too.
—VIOLET HENSLEY

The willingness to love is not easily turned off once it's been turned on. Thus, those who love freely are perhaps the luckiest people alive. Every experience they have offers them an opportunity to share love and acceptance with someone else. And ultimately, all of us reap the benefit of the love expressed by any one of us.

Seldom do we contemplate how important every tiny expression is that we make. Unconsciously, we frown rather than smile; ignore rather than acknowledge; discount rather than honor. All in the flash of an instant, we make a "contribution" to the world at large. It's awesome to acknowledge the responsibility we each have for the positive rhythms of the universe.

Let's not take our responsibility lightly. And when we realize we don't love someone all that easily, let's determine to practice. Generally, it's easy to love children and small animals. They don't intimidate us. Let's hone our skills repeatedly, starting now.

Today is a good day to give love away. Each person offers me an opportunity.

—from *Keepers of the Wisdom*

September 13

Peace can never coexist with conflict.

Do we gain anything in our many conflicts with others? We may think we do, particularly if we gain esteem from influencing others' opinions. But the pathway to that point of general agreement is often tension-filled and uncertain. There's no peace to be felt in those circumstances.

We have to decide if being peaceful appeals to us more than being right. For some, gratifying the ego takes precedence. Those people will live in perpetual conflict, perhaps never knowing that life could be experienced another way. That's their prerogative, of course. Unfortunately, because it's necessary for us to interact with myriad personalities, we'll frequently be faced with the decision to fight or take flight.

Seeing all interactions as our opportunities for moments of peacefulness lessens our dread. The decision to walk away is quite empowering. We may even begin to look for these opportunities.

Today I will focus on the benefits of creating peace.

—from *Daily Meditations for Practicing the* Course

September 14

No thought of fear can enter a mind while it thinks of God.

None of us has escaped being afraid. Some of us have been afraid most of our lives. We've tried many remedies. Alcohol and drugs may have beckoned as escapes from fear. The reprieve was short-lived, however. Meditation, visualization, and nervous prayer may also have appealed to us, leading to a modicum of success. Workaholism, illness, and an overcommitted social life have been tried by some as solutions. None of these worked for long, but there is one solution that is guaranteed. Thank goodness it's been introduced to us at last.

The solution we all have access to, in an instant, is bringing to our minds the thought of God. Sound simple? It is. It is also effective. When our minds are filled with thoughts of God, they cannot hold any other thought. Neither fear nor anger nor confusion can hinder one who dwells on God.

Does this mean we must think of nothing else? Obviously, shopping, working, and household responsibilities might carry our thoughts away. But we can return them to God when even the tiniest problem arises. What a solution!

I will be unafraid today, totally unafraid.

—from *Daily Meditations for Practicing the* Course

September 15

*The process rather than the product is primary in
caring, for it is only in the present that I can attend
to the other.*

—MILTON MAYEROFF

The moment that captures us now is all we have for certain. We can dream endlessly about next week and next year but there are no guarantees. Thus, it is important to care for ourselves and others in this moment. Have we expressed our love to any one of the many special people in our lives today? The effort is small and yet paramount in its impact on how the day unfolds for the givers and the receivers of caring words that inspire—words that speak of love.

Someone close needs our attention today—our encouragement, our inspiration, our recognition. And we need the commitment to focus outside ourselves if we are to discover the gifts promised us in each twenty-four-hour segment of life. It is not coincidence that we feel pulled toward particular people, that we select certain groups to identify with.

Contemplative thoughtfulness about our presence in this time and place will assure us we are needed for the loving growth of many. The mystery unfolds by design.

—from *Worthy of Love*

September 16

It is now clear to me that from the beginning some human beings saw that the best way of taking life was lightly.

—FLORIDA SCOTT-MAXWELL

Not overreacting to the events in our lives is a major achievement for some of us. Thinking before acting is a learned behavior; we have time and many daily opportunities to learn it.

The people who seem to laugh easily, who are always ready with encouragement, who seldom are in a personal crisis, are obvious targets of our envy. What makes them different? Why don't they struggle like we do? It isn't fair, we think.

There's just one difference between them and us: it's called faith. They have it, and we can too. Beginning each day reflecting on the Serenity Prayer will help us develop the faith we lack. Giving to God the many problems we needlessly worry over lightens our load. Laughter can come more easily to us too.

Letting God handle my problems today will allow me more time to laugh.

—from *A Woman's Spirit*

September 17

*I came to the conclusion then that "continual mind-
fulness" . . . must mean, not a sergeant-major-like
drilling of thoughts, but a continual readiness to
look and readiness to accept whatever came.*
                                    —JOANNA FIELD

Resistance to the events, the situations, the many people
who come into our lives blocks the growth we are offered
every day. Every moment of every day is offering us a gift:
the gift of awareness of other persons, awareness of our
natural surroundings, awareness of our own personal impact on creation. And in awareness comes our growth as
women.

Living in the now, being present in the moment, guarantees us the protection of God. And in the stretches of
time when we anxiously anticipate the events of the future,
we cheat ourselves of the security God offers us right now.

We are always being taken care of, right here, right now.
Being mindful, this minute, of what's happening, and
only this, eases all anxieties, erases all fears. We only struggle when we have moved our sights from the present moment. Within the now lies all peace.

*The most important lesson I have to learn, the lesson that will
eliminate all of my pain and struggle, is to receive fully that which
is offered in each moment of my life.*

—from *Each Day a New Beginning*

September 18

❧

Sharing what worked for us is far better than giving advice.

Everybody loves giving advice, but no one really loves getting it. Advice often sounds like control, and we want to be free to make our own decisions. However, we can appreciate hearing what worked for other people, and we aren't intimidated by sharing experiences. It behooves us to remember this when we are about to give advice to newcomers.

Remembering how it was for us when we first came to meetings will help us know how to approach others who are hurting as we were hurting when we first sought help. Confusion, hopelessness, and fear haunt every newcomer. The way others enfolded us in their hope when we had none made it possible to survive one day at a time. It's our turn now to pass on that hope to others.

The real gift in telling about our experiences rather than giving advice is that we too are strengthened each time we remember how far we have come.

I will be available to help a friend today. My experiences are all I really know, but that's quite enough.

—from *A Life of My Own*

September 19

Those who do not know how to weep with their whole heart don't know how to laugh either.

—GOLDA MEIR

We all know people who live on the fringes of life. They seem uninvolved with the activity in their midst, as though a pane of glass separated them from us. And there are times when we join the persons standing alone away from the vibrancy of life. Fears keep people apart, particularly the fear of letting go of the vulnerable self and joining in the feelings of the moment.

To fully reap the benefits of life, we have to risk full exposure to one another and to the experience of the moment. Full involvement in the ebb and flow of life will bring the weeping that accompanies both the pain and the joy of life. It will also bring the fruits of laughter.

Both laughter and weeping cleanse us. They bring closure to an experience. They make possible our letting go. And we must let go of pain, as well as joy, to ready ourselves for the next blessing life offers us.

When we keep ourselves apart, when we hold off the tears or the laughter, we cheat ourselves of the richness of life. We have to go through an experience fully in order to learn all it can teach us and then be free of it.

Past experiences never let me go until I fully grieve those that need to be grieved or laugh over those that deserve the light touch. The present is distorted when the past shadows it.

—from *Each Day a New Beginning*

September 20

~

*To avoid pain at all costs forces us to reject half the
lessons life can teach.*

—JAN PISHOK

If we could remember that every experience we'll ever have
is unique and offers us a lesson we will grow from, we'd accept them all with far greater ease. What's to be afraid of
anyway? God is never absent. In fact, God is present during every experience. Remembering this makes us courageous as we walk through the turmoil that interrupts the
peaceful times.

Before coming to this program, we feared most of the
situations that called to us, and understandably so. We
were often trying to do the improbable without the wisdom or the guidance that might have guaranteed success.
By taking the Third Step every morning of our lives, as has
been suggested, we can positively influence the outcome of
every experience we'll have. Hallelujah!

*I will not avoid any experience today. I'll simply remember that
God is present and that I need to know what calls to me.*

—from *A Woman's Spirit*

September 21

We can "correct" our thoughts.

Knowing that we can change our thoughts releases us from the hold any negative idea or opinion has over us. We have all heard someone lament, "I can't help how I think. It's just who I am." On the contrary, says the *Course*, we are the creators of our thoughts. We are responsible for who we are. What's good about this is that it means we can change a situation instantly by changing how we perceive it.

Some thoughts are obviously not good for us—the plan to inflict harm on someone because we aren't getting our way, for instance. Others are much more subtle, such as wishing bad luck on a friend. These thoughts might not manifest themselves in others' lives, but they do affect ours. The guilt we accumulate hinders us in all relationships. This in turn changes every experience we have.

Learning, as we presently are, that thoughts can be changed instantly gives us the tool for the kind of holy experience we truly deserve.

I will choose my thoughts wisely today. If I'm uncertain, the Holy Spirit is available for consultation.

—from *Daily Meditations for Practicing the* Course

September 22

~○

Sometimes the worst things that happen to us are the best things for us. They slow us down and make us think.

—ALICE MERRYMAN

How shortsighted we often are. We think we understand the reasons for what's happening in our lives, but that's seldom the case. Looking back on our past will reveal this, if we're open to seeing the truth. Lost treasures, failed relationships, missed opportunities devastated us when they occurred. Yet often, in only a brief lapse of time, we were able to see the folly in our disappointment. Something better was always in store for us. We simply had to make way for it; our loss opened the door.

The aging process quite often troubles us. Our health is precarious, perhaps. Our financial stability fluctuates; friends move on and loved ones die. How can any of this be good? we wonder. Let's try looking at these changes in another way. Life is change: of our bodies, our minds, our dreams, and our fears. Even a cursory review of our past reveals many changes that we dreaded when they occurred. We don't have to like them, ever, but they do help us become who we need to be. A tragedy makes us more thoughtful, perhaps, or more cautious. The death of a spouse can initiate more independence. The loss of movement due to arthritis can interest us in a new hobby to fill our time. There is always another way to see whatever is changing around us.

I will look at my experiences today from a new angle.

—from *Keepers of the Wisdom*

September 23

The Holy Spirit will solve every problem.

We all know people who seem to attract problems. Job losses follow divorces. Smashed fenders follow confrontations with friends. Perhaps we feel sorry for them. No doubt we're grateful that we don't share their experiences. Why do some people have so much turmoil?

The *Course* teaches that no one has to indefinitely endure painful circumstances. There is one solution to every dilemma: Seek the direction and comfort of the Holy Spirit and problems dissolve. Is it really as simple as it sounds? We may doubt this initially because we can't imagine our acquaintances choosing to experience such turmoil rather than seeking a simple solution. But from the *Course* we also learn about the ego who shares center stage with the Holy Spirit in one's mind. The ego isn't a problem solver in spite of its claim. On the contrary, the ego creates problems.

It's good to know that we all have equal access to the Holy Spirit. It means that none of us is destined to have more problems than others. We can all be as free of problems as we choose to be.

If I have a problem at work or with a family member or even a stranger today, I'll seek the right solution.

—from *Daily Meditations for Practicing the* Course

September 24

Is there ever any particular spot where one can put one's finger and say, "It all began that day, at such a time and such a place, with such an incident"?

—AGATHA CHRISTIE

No experience of our lives is pure, unadulterated, set apart from all other experiences. There is an eternal flow in our lives. It carries us from one moment, one experience, into the next. Where we are today, the growth we have attained as recovering women and the plans we have for further changes are prompted by the same driving desires that contributed to our many actions in years gone by.

We can reflect on a particular experience and tag it a turning point. However, neither a lone prescription nor a single martini opened the door we passed through when we chose recovery. But they each may have played a part, and it's the many parts of our lives, past and present, that guarantee us the turning points that nudge us further up the mountain. We will see the summit. And we will understand how, each time we stumbled, new strength was gained.

Every day is a training ground. And every experience trains me to recognize the value of succeeding experiences. With richness, I am developing, one moment at a time.

—from *Each Day a New Beginning*

September 25

No experience is without meaning.

Often we assume that the experiences we want are the most important ones for our development as human beings. But that may not be the case at all. Experiences that seem insignificant at the time, or ones that are not at all what we want, might prove to be key to our future growth. We are unfolding purposefully. Where today's experience takes us is quite by design.

Most of us wish that at least some things could be different. Maybe we think we deserve a better job or a happier, sober marriage. Maybe our children rarely live up to our high expectations. We get trapped into thinking we deserve better. And perhaps we are getting a heavy share of tough experiences to handle. But God is always with us, and everything that comes to us is intended to contribute to the person we are becoming.

Our perspective can lead to appreciation or dread. Deciding to see every situation as a blessing could significantly change us and what happens in our lives.

I am living an adventure today. God will give me experiences that I need. I may want other experiences, but God's love guarantees I'll get what I need.

—from *A Life of My Own*

September 26

Every experience has something to teach us.

We're students every minute. And as a result, *we teach*. Even in the most difficult struggles, we're storing information that will help us or someone else at a future time. From our happy times as well as our tragedies we gain valuable, necessary insights.

We probably didn't know this when we first came into the program. And we may still forget it regularly. Fortunately, we are surrounded by people who help us remember that every experience has a purpose. Each journey is unique, and the lessons in every experience are by design and on schedule. God's plan for us has brought us here. God's plan for our future will take us wherever we need to be.

Our fears diminish when we know that God is in charge and that our journey is according to Divine design. Our assignment is simply to listen and learn and pass on to others what we've been taught.

What my experiences teach me today, God intends for me to learn. I'll look for the opportunity to share what I know with someone else.

—from *A Life of My Own*

September 27

When I met Harry, I knew immediately we should be together.

—EDITH HUEY BARTHOLOMEW

Listening to our inner voice changes how we see the events in our lives. It won't steer us wrong. Our ability to decipher the message, to not confuse the "advice" that comes from the ego with the wisdom that comes from our inner voice, is what we have to perfect. The ego can sound very wise. It has practiced its art for as many years as we have been alive. But its advice is always meant to keep us hostage to it. We're not well served by the ego.

The wisdom that arises from our inner voice does nothing but serve our better interests. It fosters love in our hearts. It ushers us toward individuals who need us as much as we need them. It makes us willing to forgive the transgressions of others, helping us to know that another's actions always grew out of fear. The inner voice is God's messenger. It speaks ever so softly, but if we are attentive, we will hear it.

Edith seemingly heard the "messenger" when she met Harry in her later life. He showered her with love and devotion. He inspired her to continue her work as a nature photographer. Their companionship changed the world as perceived by each of them. Let's listen to our inner voice and relish the surprise that might be in store for us.

My inner voice will show me the way to proceed today. It will never lead me astray.

—from *Keepers of the Wisdom*

September 28

How important is it?

Impulsively we get into conflicts because we don't stop and think first. If a friend is about to do something her way, rather than our way, we often want to interfere. How much simpler we'd make our lives if we'd ask ourselves, "How important is it anyway?"

No two of us share the same perception of any situation, and each of us is certain our perception is right. That leads us to meaningless conflicts. Most disagreements are irrelevant, at least in the "big picture." Why, then, must we participate in them? The good news is, we don't have to. "How important is it anyway?" gives us a moment's pause, and that's generally all we need to walk away.

Minding our own business would profoundly change our experiences. We'd soon discover that we had extra time to pursue personal goals if we gave up watchdogging everyone else.

Any conflict I get into is because I've forgotten to ask the simple question, "How important is it anyway?" I'll be mindful of this today and stop myself before I get into conflict.

—from *A Life of My Own*

September 29

Love has a hundred gentle ends.
—LEONORA SPEYER

Letting go is a process that is seldom easy. For many, its meaning is elusive. How do we "let go"? Letting go means removing our attention from a particular experience or person and putting our focus on the here and now. We hang on to the past, to past hurts, but also to past joys. We have to let the past pass. The struggle to hang on to it, any part of it, clouds the present. You can't see the possibilities today is offering if your mind is still drawn to what was.

Letting go can be a gentle process. Our trust in our higher power and our faith that good will prevail, in spite of appearances, eases the process. And we must let each experience end, as its moment passes, whether it is good or bad, love or sorrow. It helps to remember that all experiences contribute to our growth and wholeness. No experience will be ignored by the inner self who is charting our course. All are parts of the journey. And every moment has a gentle end, but no moment is forgotten.

My journey today is akin to yesterday's journey and tomorrow's too. I will savor each moment and be ready for the next.

—from *Each Day a New Beginning*

September 30

We can't give our thoughts away.

Our thoughts determine who we are. We may want to push thoughts on others, and no doubt try. But they are still ours. What we can do, however, is change our thoughts. We never have to keep holding a thought we don't want.

Let's say we think a friend has been disparaging us behind our back. We are obsessed with worry and maybe anger. We're afraid of a confrontation, so we keep mulling it over in our minds. How can we get beyond this thought short of approaching our friend? Not surprisingly, the *Course* has a solution: Recognize that thoughts which "attack," whether real or imagined, are a call for love.

Perhaps we aren't willing to offer love or forgiveness when we feel someone has hurt us, but we can decide to give up our own attack thoughts with the help of God. We give them up in the process of changing them, and we change them by asking for a better vision of the situation. A more positive perspective may not come immediately, but that's because the ego still wields control. Be patient and ask again.

I will look at what I'm thinking today and make better choices if I'm not happy.

—from *Daily Meditations for Practicing the* Course

October

October 1

An active listener is to be prized above rubies.
—RUTH HUMLECKER

Giving our undivided attention to a friend can be difficult. Even though we care deeply for her and value her friendship, we often find it hard to keep our own thoughts from intruding. As she talks, we take note of other people in the vicinity. We think about the tasks we have yet to complete. And we may pass judgment on what she shares.

Letting go of having these kinds of thoughts while in conversation with a friend is hard, but it's worth the work. No encounter is an accident, and every exchange with a friend or even a stranger has its reward for us. We are God's students every moment.

When we listen, we learn how to handle situations we might face in the future. We learn to show respect through our caring attention. We grow in our understanding of the value of friendship. Perhaps most important, we learn the value of cultivating a quiet mind. Only a quiet mind can hear the words of our Higher Power coming through the gentle voice of a friend.

I will be an active listener today. I am ready to learn whatever God has in store for me.

—from *A Woman's Spirit*

October 2

God's voice can be heard above any noise.

Taking time for prayer and meditation is advantageous to everyone. Their importance is lost on no one. Why don't we practice them regularly? The most common excuse is that we are running late and don't have time. Aren't we lucky to have discovered that we needn't take time? We can seek and gain God's wisdom and guidance no matter where we are or what we are doing. We can be in the middle of a conference, a painful confrontation, a job interview, or a tennis game, and God will acknowledge our request for guidance.

Being assured of this is one of the great lessons of life. Too bad it takes so long to learn it, but each time we are saved from a disaster, we sense that a guiding hand was present. We'd profit more if we acknowledged Its presence more often. It's comforting to know that we'll always have the help we need to survive any experience. After all, the situations we encounter are nothing more than our schooling. The best Teacher is only a thought away.

Nothing I do today is unseen by the Holy Spirit. If I'm having trouble I can ask for help.

—from *Daily Meditations for Practicing the* Course

October 3

The truest measurement of my growth and
accomplishments is in remembering where I
came from, where I've been, and where I'm going.
—JOAN ROHDE

Our daily routines can be so absorbing that we lose perspective on how we used to live. That's okay. We need to be present to the moment. However, it benefits us to remember occasionally what our lives used to be like. Never getting too far from the insanity of our past helps us be grateful for the gifts that have become commonplace now.

We've grown as the result of recovery. For many of us, very little in our lives looks or feels the same. We have new friends, sober relationships, more self-esteem, and a positive direction.

A true gift of this new life is that we have hope. We know we can do great things. We know we lived through our traumas because we had not yet fulfilled our purpose, our part of God's destiny. And we know we'll get the guidance we need to fulfill that destiny if we remain committed to the program's principles.

I am in a "growing" state of mind. My life is a rich and purposeful play directed by my Higher Power.

—from *A Woman's Spirit*

October 4

*There's a period of life where we swallow a
knowledge of ourselves and it becomes either good
or sour inside.*

—PEARL BAILEY

For too many of us, feelings of shame, even self-hatred,
are paramount. No one of us has a fully untarnished past.
Every man, every woman, even every child experiences regret over some action. We are not perfect. Perfection is not
expected in the Divine plan. But we are expected to take
our experiences and grow from them, to move beyond the
shame of them, to celebrate what they have taught us.

Each day offers us a fresh start at assimilating all that
we have been. What has gone before enriches who we are
now, and through the many experiences we've survived,
we have been prepared to help others, to smooth the way
for another woman, perhaps, who is searching for new
direction.

We can let go of our shame and know instead that it
sweetens the nuggets of the wisdom we can offer to others.
We are alike. We are not without faults. Our trials help another to smoother sailing.

*I will relish the joy at hand. I can share my wisdom. All painful
pasts brighten someone's future, when openly shared.*

—from *Each Day a New Beginning*

October 5

*Being willing to listen wholly is a quality worth
striving for.*

Our preoccupation with silent, ongoing dialogues about
"what she said yesterday" or "what he may do later today"
prevents us from *hearing* what a friend may be trying to tell
us now. And it's our struggle to control the "hims and
hers" in our lives that keeps us focused on the other person even when that person isn't present. The obsession to
control gets in the way of our sanity and serenity. We miss
living with our *own* lives when we obsessively focus on how
the significant people in our lives are living theirs.

We have heard at Twelve Step meetings that frequently
our Higher Power's guidance comes to us through the loving words of friends. If we are not listening intently while
in conversation with our friends, we will miss the message God has for us. That message is exactly what we need
right now.

*I will focus on my friends today and listen. Their words contain
the thoughts that should come to me.*

—from *A Life of My Own*

October 6

Simplicity and greatness go together.
—MONTY CRALLEY

We have probably heard the phrase *Keep It Simple* thousands of times. It's possible we are mystified by it, even yet. So many things in life have seemed complicated: getting an education, starting a new job, advising children and friends. Not many things can be pursued without careful consideration. When we have approached situations carelessly, we have often blundered badly.

Keeping it simple means doing only the next right thing, not a sequence of fourteen things all at once. To keep something simple means to focus on only a tiny bit of the problem at a time. If we employ a little hindsight, we'll quickly recall how many situations began to improve as we attended to just a portion of them.

God never gives us more than we can handle. How many times have we heard that? It means we'll always be shown the way to handle something little by little, *very simply*, in exactly the order we need the information. Don't we see this is how it has always been? Why would it change now?

Today I need to listen. I don't need to figure out all my problems at once.

—from *Keepers of the Wisdom*

October 7

Imagination grows by exercise and, contrary to
common belief, is more powerful in the mature
than in the young.

—W. SOMERSET MAUGHAM

Children are uninhibited. They speak their truth quite
openly, at least until their elders redefine it for them. From
that moment forth, they, as we before them, see through
the lenses of others. It took most of us until adulthood to
rediscover our own truths. And even now, we aren't always
brave enough to speak them.

Perhaps the greatest gift of maturity is freedom to do
what we want when we want and having the willingness
to dare to believe whatever pleases us. We really don't have
to live according to someone else's standards any longer.
As long as we don't harm another, we can believe what we
want, do what we want, imagine what we want. And the
earlier we matured, the spicier our imaginations.

A major benefit of old age is letting our minds wander
to far-off places and not having to account for the lost
hours. We've earned our freedom. Let's share our joy with
one who is still maturing.

*I have paid my dues. I am free to wonder or wander. This day will
be as rich and full as I make it.*

—from *Keepers of the Wisdom*

October 8

Relish life, one moment at a time.

Why is it so hard to do the very thing that would make life feel so much softer and more manageable? Most of our worries relate to what may happen in our future, and our regrets are over what has happened in our past. Between our worries and our regrets, we leave little time for our minds to rest and relish the flavors of the present.

Reliving past traumas and projecting future ones tire us almost as much as the actual experiences. We gain nothing from our obsession to dwell on the past and the future. In fact, we lose a lot. We lose the message our Higher Power is trying to give us through the *present* experience when that experience does not capture our full attention.

In the present we get all our answers. In the present we find security and hope. In the present we get well.

I will bring my attention back to now every time it wanders today. I'll feel my Higher Power's presence.

—from *A Life of My Own*

October 9

Giving love reinforces it.

Most of the agitation any of us feel stems from the belief that we aren't getting what we want and think we deserve. More money, more possessions, more friends, more love, more happiness. Seldom do we focus on what we may be giving to others; rather, we notice what they aren't giving to us!

It's true that some people will always have more material wealth than us and others will have less. However, when it comes to peace of mind, we may selfishly hang on to what we think makes us happy—a relationship or our job status—fearing its disappearance. The paradox is that we do lose what we so stingily hang on to.

It's a radical change of perspective to focus on what we give. We are so used to assessing what we are given, and we judge a person's value accordingly. None of us would deny that we'd like more peace and love in our lives. That's easy to decide. The reality is that we can get exactly that as quick as a flash. All we have to do is give away what we want. It will come back to us.

What I get today I have asked for by my actions.

—from *Daily Meditations for Practicing the* Course

October 10

*When I'm acting as if I'm the center of the universe,
it's helpful to be reminded that I'm just another
bozo on the bus.*

—ROSE CASEY

Being just another bozo on the bus doesn't mean that our
lives lack importance. On the contrary, we are coming to
believe that each of us is here by design and destined to
make a unique contribution to the whole of humankind.
We are also coming to understand that our participation
in an unfolding situation does not affect its entire outcome, crucial though our part may be.

When we can fully understand the meaning of this
truth, we will sense a freedom that we did not know before. In the past we tried to be the center of the universe.
This meant being responsible for nearly every circumstance affecting almost everyone we knew. Through the
program we are learning that being in charge of ourselves,
and ourselves only, is a big enough job in itself. Freeing
ourselves of the burden of making decisions for everyone
we love will enhance our well-being. Let's revel in our
bozoness!

*I am as free and as joyful as I want to be today. I am in charge of
myself and my well-being.*

—from *A Woman's Spirit*

October 11

One of the many blessings or opportunities my recovery gives me is the realization that there is a bus out of the old neighborhood.

—ELIZABETH FARRELL

Today we have many opportunities to chart a new course in our behavior. We don't have to keep feeling inadequate or anxious. We can decide to change how we act toward other people and how we respond to the unexpected. It's our choice.

There is great hope and promise in knowing how personally responsible we are for our actions and, thus, our successes. There is even greater hope in knowing that we can feel as peaceful as we make up our minds to feel. With our Higher Power's help, we are in charge of the way we see the events in our lives. And with that help we are in charge of how we maneuver through the moments of every day. What lucky women we are! Never again will we be at the mercy of our obsessive feelings. And never again will life be any more difficult than we decide to let it be. With the help of each other, our Higher Power, and our willingness to change, we will know a new freedom.

I can hop on the bus of change at any stop throughout the day. And it's a free ride to serenity!

—from *A Woman's Spirit*

October 12

*True intimacy with another human being can only
be experienced when you have found true peace
within yourself.*

—ANGELA L. WOZNIAK

Intimacy means disclosure—full expression of ourselves to
another person. Nothing held back. All bared. There are
risks, of course: rejection, criticism, perhaps ridicule. But
the comfort we feel within is directly proportional to the
peace we've come to know.

Each day we commit ourselves to recovery, we find a
little more peace. Each conversation we have with our
higher power brings us a little more security. Each time we
turn our full attention to another person's needs, we feel
our own burdens lightened.

Peace comes in stages. As we continue to accept our
powerlessness, the depth of our peace increases. Turning
more often to a power greater than ourselves eases our
resistance to whatever condition prevails. Forgiving ourselves and others, daily, heightens our appreciation of all
life and enhances our humility. Therein lies peace.

We each are a necessary part of the creative spirit pre-
vailing in this world. The details of our lives are well in
hand. We can be at peace. Who we are is who we need to be.

*Intimacy lets me help someone else also live a full and peace-filled
life. I will reach out to someone today.*

—from Each Day a New Beginning

October 13

～

Codependency was a survival tactic.

Are we troubled because we often bear the brunt of someone's anger but say nothing? Do we frequently adjust what we think or say in order to get along better with someone else? If we are guilty of either, then we may be suffering from *codependency,* a condition for which there is a powerful antidote.

It's not unusual to grow up worrying about and reacting to the feelings of others while stuffing our own feelings. Most of us have suffered guilt and shame as forms of discipline. We learned to align our feelings and opinions with those around us as a survival tactic. But we never felt good about it because it never felt honest. Even worse, our self-esteem languished.

The Fourth Step helps us define who we are. The more open and honest we become, the less willing we'll be to let others treat us unjustly. Knowing our values will empower us to share them. Sharing them will free us from codependency.

I don't have to be silent if mistreated. Today I will not harbor resentment; instead, I will express my feelings.

—from *A Life of My Own*

October 14

Some of my grandchildren say they want to be like me. That's a wonderful compliment.

—ALICE MERRYMAN

It's likely we have all been role models for someone. Certainly we can look back on our own lives and recall those individuals we hoped to imitate. We probably made a few wrong choices along the way, too. That's not uncommon, nor irreparable. Those who have looked up to us might have taken with them some of our less attractive traits as well. We aren't responsible for what others have noticed and copied, but we are responsible for what we copied in others.

Are we still "forming" ourselves, or have we "arrived"? There's no simple answer. By this age, we hope to have settled on certain traits we'd rather not lose, but the more thoughtful among us realize that making select changes in our behaviors and attitudes can go on endlessly. *We're not done until we are done.* There's real excitement in that idea. It means ongoing growth and new experiences. Every time we change something, it impacts many other areas of our lives as well as others. Change engages us, and that's what life is about.

Watching others watch us will keep us on our toes. Let's not send someone away with one of the traits that we're ashamed of. Let's put our best self forward.

Do my friends and offspring think well of me? Yesterday's impressions aren't necessarily today's.

—from *Keepers of the Wisdom*

October 15

~☞

Love cures. It cures those who give it and cures those who receive it.

—DR. KARL MENNINGER

We are making a response to life every waking moment; our attitudes formulate the tenor of our responses. When the sun warms our bodies and the flowers tease our nostrils, it may be easy to love everyone and smile. When we have a negative attitude, we may snarl and all too quickly criticize innocent bystanders, as well as friends and family. All we need is to make a simple decision to look with love as far as our eyes can see.

When our hearts are God-centered and filled with love and laughter, we'll find no experience too difficult to handle. No problem will evade its solution for long.

An attitude of love promises us gratitude in abundance. We'll never doubt that all is well when love is at our center.

—from *Worthy of Love*

October 16

Our agitation can easily be dissolved.

The tension of agitation exhilarates us on occasion. We may even like the feeling. Its outcome seldom satisfies us, however. Being at odds with others frequently escalates tension beyond our tolerance level. And then what?

The short-term gratification we may get from cursory agitation doesn't feel good for long. So often we feel stuck with it, but that's never actually the case. We can be free of it instantly. We can just as quickly grab it back, of course.

The challenge of finding a peaceful path seems overwhelming many days. It's interesting that we find it harder to choose peace rather than turmoil. Only when we understand how insistent and persistent the ego is about controlling us can we in turn fathom the seriousness of our struggle. The ego never has to win, however. That's up to us.

I will be at peace today if that's my choice.

—from *Daily Meditations for Practicing the* Course

October 17

The most important thing we are doing right now is
thinking nice thoughts.
—JIM AND MARIE BURNS

Just thinking nice thoughts sounds so simplistic, doesn't
it? Surely there is more in life to contemplate than that.
But the power of nice thoughts, the impact just such a
simple decision can have on our lives and the lives of everyone in our company, is awesome. Having nice thoughts
and only nice thoughts is a significant departure for most
of us. Far more commonly we quietly or vocally judged
every man, woman, and child in our presence. Stopping
ourselves from judging, in fact, stopping a judgment in its
tracks, will reveal how swamped our thinking has been by
the critical, mean-spirited side of us.

Seldom do we cultivate a quiet, peaceful mind. Seemingly out of control, our minds race from one idea, one
judgment, one negative opinion to another one of equal
harm to ourselves and the entire human community. Perhaps we didn't realize that every thought we harbor has an
impact, whether it's voiced aloud or not. We can't lay the
blame for this violent, mean world solely on others. We've
had a part in it, too. Every time we favor a nasty thought
rather than a nice thought, we add to the turmoil around
us. The good news is that we can choose between the two
at will.

I will add to the tenor of the world today by my thoughts. I pray
that I may choose them carefully.

—from Keepers of the Wisdom

October 18

Wisdom comes wrapped in many packages.

Nearly every day we ponder what to do about a nagging situation. We review in our minds the "he saids, she saids" until we're worn out, oftentimes still troubled about what to do. And then we remember we have guiding voices all around us.

What lucky people we are. If it weren't for the role chemical dependency has played in our lives, we might never have known that a Higher Power was present to help us. Nor would we have known that a passage in a special book held a message for us. Or that the friends we've met in the program really care about our well-being and that their suggestions can be trusted.

Wisdom will come to us when we are ready for it. When the student is ready, the teacher appears.

I will listen to my teachers today. No situation has to baffle me.

—from *A Life of My Own*

October 19

❧

*Parents can only give good advice or put them on
the right paths, but the final forming of a person's
character lies in their own hands.*

—ANNE FRANK

We must take responsibility for ourselves, for who we become, for how we live each day. The temptation to blame others may be ever present. And much of our past adds up to wasted days or years perhaps, because we did blame someone else for the unhappiness in our lives.

We may have blamed our own parents for not loving us enough. We may have labeled our husbands the villains. Other people did affect us. That's true. However, we chose, you and I, to let them control us, overwhelm us, shame us. We always had other options, but we didn't choose them.

Today is a new day. Recovery has opened up our options. We are learning who we are and how we want to live our lives. How exhilarating to know that you and I can take today and put our own special flavor in it. We can meet our personal needs. We can, with anticipation, chart our course. The days of passivity are over, if we choose to move ahead with this day.

I will look to this day. Every day is a new beginning.

—from *Each Day a New Beginning*

October 20

*Sometimes the things that frighten you the most can
turn out to be the biggest sources of strength.*

—IRIS TIMBERLAKE

Not many things would send fear through us if we remembered to rely on our Higher Power at all times. Yet we try to handle circumstances ourselves first. It's often only when we finally feel hopeless that we turn to our Higher Power for the help that awaited us all along.

We make our lives much more difficult than they need to be. Let's quit thinking through our problems alone, no matter how foolish they seem. Let's quit trying to handle tough people alone. Let's trust that every circumstance, no matter how small, is a lesson offered by God. And let's know that the outcome will be the right one for our particular growth at that moment.

Things that frighten us do so only because we have failed to remember the presence of our Higher Power. Let's pray for the willingness to remember God's presence. When we do, we will know a new strength.

Today I will let God help me handle every moment of my day.

—from *A Woman's Spirit*

October 21

Let's begin where we are.

We're seeking to understand our purpose here. We're told this world is our classroom. Does the pain and confusion we feel much of the time mean we're deserving of punishment? Of course not, but the guilt comes so naturally to us; it's difficult to shake these fears about ourselves. It's comforting to hear that we're always where we need to be even when we don't understand what this means.

Our return to God, which is the intent of our journey, is our ultimate destination. Every one of us has this same destination, the same, underlying purpose here. However, we all take steps, learn specifics, encounter experiences that are unique to only us. And we have to pass through the circumstances that call to us when the time is right, when our time has come.

We may not be able to account for many situations today. They won't seem to fit with what happened yesterday. The best attitude to cultivate is one of gentle indifference. We are where we are needed. We'll arrive when our journey is done.

I need not think beyond the next moment. Today is taken care of.

—from *Daily Meditations for Practicing the* Course

October 22

We can choose to have no cares, no worries, no anxieties.

This seems like a frivolous wish. To believe that it's a choice seems highly improbable. How can we not worry about our children, marriages, and jobs? To believe we want to worry seems ridiculous, but that's the truth. Many don't accept this idea quickly, but we all will if we follow the suggestion offered in the *Course*.

This suggestion is so simple, so tiny, and so subtle that it doesn't seem like it could affect anything. At first it seems like we're in denial about our problems, but we're in for a big and pleasant surprise. The *Course* says, think and act with the help of the Holy Spirit. Regardless of what the ego tells us, we can see ourselves joined with "the adversaries." We can see their anger or attack or control as a request for healing and help, nothing more. We can answer them with love. Nothing more. And our lives will change forever.

I'll make whatever choice I want to make today. Worries don't just happen.

—from *Daily Meditations for Practicing the* Course

October 23

The most important ingredient for a long life is having something you really want to do.

—EVA WINES

We all have acquaintances who complain bitterly about their lives. They feel forgotten by their children. Their health may be failing. Money is scarce. They see nothing to look forward to. The state of the world disturbs them. They aren't a lot of fun to be around, but perhaps they serve as good reminders of who we don't want to be. Our teachers are everywhere, we are told.

It's important to monitor how we greet each new day. Is it with welcome anticipation or do we drag ourselves out of bed? If it's the latter, we'd better try something new. Boredom is deadly and there's no good reason for any of us to suffer from it. Libraries are overflowing with books we haven't read about ideas we haven't ever considered. Community centers are filled with people seeking the company of people like ourselves. On every block is a man or woman who would love to share the passion they feel for a hobby they have pursued. All we have to do is be willing to make ourselves available for any one of these options.

Living a long life may not be your goal. And that's okay. But living peacefully for whatever amount of time remains is certainly a preference we can all relate to. How are you doing?

What do I want from this next twenty-four hours? I can have it. What a marvelous gift.

—from *Keepers of the Wisdom*

October 24

~○

Problems are opportunities for stretching our minds.

Wringing our hands over circumstances gone awry wastes our energy. In any twenty-four hours we will experience many situations that will evolve according to God's plan, rather than our own. We'd feel our spirits being lifted if we could assume that any ripple in a day's activities is simply God's way of reminding us that outcomes are not ours to orchestrate.

As we grow accustomed to a broader range of perspectives than just our own, we become more aware of the multiplicity of views. This stretches our minds, teaching us to see in new and valuable ways. It is no accident that each of us brings a unique contribution and personal viewpoint to the table. God's design has gathered us together to learn from one another.

I will appreciate other people's viewpoints today. It is part of God's plan for my growth.

—from *A Life of My Own*

▸

October 25

❧

It is good to have an end to journey towards; but it
is the journey that matters, in the end.
—URSULA K. LE GUIN

Goals give direction to our lives. We need to know who we
are and where we want to go. But the trip itself, the steps
we travel, offer us daily satisfaction moment by moment—
fulfillment, if we'd but realize it. Too often we keep our
sights on the goal's completion, rather than the process—
the day-to-day living that makes the completion possible.

How often do we think, "When I finish college, I'll feel
stronger." Or, "After the divorce is final, I can get back to
work." Or even, "When I land that promotion, my troubles
are over." Life will begin "when"—or so it seems in our
minds. And when this attitude controls our thinking, we
pass up our opportunity to live, altogether.

Looking back on goals already completed in our lives,
what so quickly follows the end of a job well done is a let-
down. And how sad that the hours, the days, the weeks,
maybe even the months we toiled are gone, with little
sense of all they could have meant.

I will not forget that every moment of every day I can be God-
centered and joyous. The goal I'm striving toward will carry with
it a special gift; it will offer the growing person within me an extra
thrill, if I've attended to the journey as much as its end.

—from *Each Day a New Beginning*

October 26

My children have a Higher Power, and it's not me.
—CAROLYN WHITE

We all have certain people in our lives, whether they are adults or children, who we think would fare better if they followed our will. Discovering that everyone has a Higher Power, one of the first lessons of recovery, relieves us of a heavy burden. It means we aren't to blame for what anyone else chooses to do. Of course, we can't take credit for their successes either.

What would make us want to assume responsibility for how others live? Surely we all have enough to do in our own lives. Perhaps our insecurity drives us to try to control others. We fear their actions won't include consideration of us unless we interfere. Fortunately, our interference is seldom successful. If it were, our lives would be far more complicated. Crisis would be far more prevalent.

I will focus on my life and my Higher Power today. Others' actions are not my responsibility.

—from *A Woman's Spirit*

October 27

Lifelong relationships aren't always smooth.

It's common for individuals to discard relationships that aren't pleasant. In terms of the *Course,* however, we are attracted to learning partners by design. Leaving a hostile relationship probably means working out that same struggle with someone else, some other time. It's not wrong to decide to leave, but let's not assume there's no lesson in every encounter.

Looking at relationships from this perspective removes the fear about them. Acknowledging that conflict is due to the ego's selfishness makes it possible to understand its attempt to control. We come to believe that we need not get along beautifully every minute of the day for a relationship to be lifelong and meaningful. The desire to join as One in spirit and love rather than fight as separate, hateful human beings is reason enough to open our hands to the Holy Spirit each time some tension ensues.

I don't have to be happy every minute to stay in a relationship. I will take note of the opportunities to see beyond the struggles today.

—from *Daily Meditations for Practicing the* Course

October 28

Even on a rainy day, I can feel the sunshine.
Even when the clouds are gray, I can feel a glow.
There's a little light inside me, just keeps burning.
I take it with me, everywhere I go.

—JILL CLARK

We carry within ourselves the single necessary ingredient for our happiness: a positive attitude. Nothing can ruin our day, unless we let it. No remark can devastate us, unless we let it. No person can have a harmful, lasting impact on us, unless we let him or her. No unhealthy, negative attitude controls our thoughts without our assent.

Feeling good about the experiences we're having, regardless of their nature, is a decision. Trusting that some good will come out of every one of them is a habit we can form. We can acquire an attitude of hope for growth and positive change.

I will see the sunshine even through the clouds if that's my choice. Today I have twenty-four hours to practice this.

—from *A Woman's Spirit*

October 29

. . . I was taught that the way of progress is neither swift nor easy.

—MARIE CURIE

We are looking for progress, not perfection; however, we sometimes get lost or confused between the two. Expecting ourselves to be perfect at something we are only now learning is a familiar affliction. As we accept our humanness, we'll allow the mistakes that are a normal part of the process of living and learning—a process we call progress.

Our need to be perfect will lessen with time. And we can help ourselves break the old habits. Perfection and self-worth are not symbiotic, except in our minds. And it's a symbiosis that has done us a grave injustice. Breaking the old thought patterns takes a commitment. We must first decide and believe that we are worthwhile, simply because we are. There is only one of us; we have a particular gift to offer this world. And our being is perfect as is. Affirming this, repeatedly, is our beginning. But with this, too, progress will be slow; perfection need only be worked for, not achieved.

The patterns I am weaving with my life are complex, full of intricate detail and knots. I need to go slow, taking only one stitch at a time. With hindsight I will see that whatever the progress, it was the perfect fit to the overall design.

—from *Each Day a New Beginning*

October 30

Taking appropriate action becomes easier with practice.

Whether we *act* or *react* can have a profound impact on our lives. Letting someone's drinking, irritability, or depression take charge of our own feelings and behavior means having a less than satisfactory life at best. And many of us had lives of reactionary desperation before our introduction to this Twelve Step program.

At first we may not understand the difference between *acting* and *reacting*. Perhaps the easiest way to discern the difference is by how we feel. We feel empowered by our carefully selected responses to a situation—by acting. We feel drained, powerless, and oftentimes hopeless by an emotional and irrational response—by reacting.

Fortunately, we can learn to quit reacting. Taking a ten- or fifteen-second pause before making a move will keep us in charge of what we do.

Many times today I'll be on the verge of reacting when I could act instead. I pray to remember to pause.

—from *A Life of My Own*

October 31

We all have a place to fill or we wouldn't be here. That's what I think.

—ALICE MERRYMAN

What do you think about your presence in this life, this neighborhood, this family and collection of friends? Do you chalk up your experiences to coincidence or have they been "chosen" lessons wearing your particular name? Believing, as Alice does, can be comforting. It can offer us freedom from grief and resentment if our lives have been filled with turmoil. But beware; this philosophy doesn't mean the turmoil goes away. It only means we could grow from it if we want to.

Obviously, we are still here. According to Alice, this can mean only one thing: We aren't done yet. Our services are still needed by someone. Must we know who? Not really, but we may be able to figure it out by listening intently to the people who reach out to us. Chances are, we'll have ample opportunities to respond to other people today. They may be the reason we're still here, in fact.

This makes one's life pretty exciting, doesn't it? It's like every moment is a mystery and we have a part in solving it. Just knowing we are truly needed can change one's outlook instantly. Maybe we didn't believe this before, but that's okay. Old dogs can learn new tricks.

Am I using my time as well as I can today?

—from *Keepers of the Wisdom*

November

November 1

Listening is a gift to ourselves.

Why is it so hard to really listen? Perhaps one reason is that for decades people have been talking *at* us rather than *with* us. Parents, teachers, friends, bosses, lovers, or spouses have offered us years of accumulated talk. But how much of this talk have we really let in?

Listening is valuable. What the people around us communicate can beckon us to the growth that is necessary to fulfill our purpose here. Even when we don't want to hear what they have to say, their words can trigger insight and new direction for us, and can deepen our understanding of our journey.

Most of us get an occasional glimpse of our purpose in this life, and when it comes we feel radiant, uplifted. But mostly we have to trust that God is showing us the way even if we don't see it. That's where listening to other people helps. They can be the messengers of our Higher Power.

I will remember that God is revealing my purpose through the men and women talking to me today. I will listen.

—from *A Life of My Own*

November 2

You must do the thing you think you cannot do.
—ELEANOR ROOSEVELT

How can we ever do that which seems impossible? Taking a class, quitting a job, leaving a destructive relationship behind, asking for help; none of these can we do alone or with ease. All of these we can handle when we rely on the help offered by the program, the help of one another, the help promised by our higher power. Tackling with God's help that which seems impossible reduces it to manageable size. It also deflates the power our fears have given it.

That which we fear grows in proportion to our obsession with it. The more we fear a thing, the bigger it becomes, which in turn increases our fear. How lucky we are that God awaits our call for the strength, the companionship that is guaranteed us! We are in partnership, all the way, every day, if we'd only recognize it. We can move toward and through anything. And the added benefit is that we come to trust our partnership. We soon know that all situations can be met. All experiences can be survived. Avoidance is no longer our technique for survival.

A deep breath invites the inner strength to move through me. I will feel the exhilaration of God's power. And I will know the excitement of growth and peace.

—from *Each Day a New Beginning*

November 3

*When we are all wrapped up in ourselves, we
present a very small package to others.*
— GEORGETTE VICKSTROM

Self-centeredness affects many people, not just recovering
women. In this program, we are honing the skills that can
free us from its clutches. Being willing to use these skills is
the hallmark of our recovery.

Everybody on our path today needs our attention. Each
person we meet may have something to teach us, or perhaps the reverse is true. But if we are focused on ourselves
we'll miss these opportunities. Being open to other people
helps us grow. If our attention is forever inward, we'll
never grow beyond our current limited understanding.

Let's be willing to give more of ourselves to others
today. The benefits we'll reap will move us forward in our
personal journey.

*Today I can put aside my tendency to look at every circumstance
in relationship to myself. With God's help, I can put my attention
on others.*

—from *A Woman's Spirit*

November 4

Problems are not as we see them.

Our perspective determines our interpretation of an experience. What amuses one person may anger a second and edify a third. Thus we may wonder how we are ever to get along with other people. Differing perspectives give rise to simple disagreement, major dysfunction, and at the extreme, violence and war. We see the evidence everywhere.

So what does it mean to say problems are not as we see them? Well, if we realize that each person sees each situation differently we begin to see that no problem is definite or absolute in scope. It is possible to see problems from a different perspective if we're willing to stretch our minds.

How do we stretch our minds? It's rather easy. We go to the quiet space within for a different view of that which troubles us. If our request is sincere, and our willingness genuine, we'll find that which we seek.

If I don't like what I see today, it's up to me to seek a different view.

—from *Daily Meditations for Practicing the* Course

November 5

We are who we are, shaped and molded by the times, by the events, and by the persons we encounter on our way, and no one ever changes very much or escapes entirely from that mold.
—RUTH CASEY

Everything we experience today is woven with all that has gone before. We are a tapestry in progress. We grow and change, heightening some of our patterns, successfully diminishing others, and maintaining still others. We need feel no shame for this person we've become; we've done our best. From this point forward, with the help of the program, our Higher Power, and the wonderful friendships that sustain us, we will add many new colors and stronger threads to the tapestry that continues to be us.

Even though there is often much we want to change in ourselves, there is much that will and should stay the same. Let's trust that God will guide our efforts in changing those traits that deserve our attention now, leaving the rest for another time. We have been loved, guided, and protected even though we are not perfect. That will be true always.

All that has gone before will help me handle whatever today offers. I am in God's keeping now and forever.

—from *A Woman's Spirit*

November 6

Fortuitous circumstances constitute the moulds that shape the majority of human lives.

—AUGUSTA EVANS

Being in the right place at the right time is how we generally explain our good fortune or the good fortune of a friend. But it's to our advantage to understand how we managed to be in the right place at just the right moment.

We have probably heard many times at meetings that God's timetable is not necessarily the same as our timetable. That events will happen as scheduled to fit a picture bigger than the picture encompassed by our egos. And frequently our patience wears thin because we aren't privy to God's timetable. But we can trust, today and always, that doors open on time. Opportunities are offered when we are ready for them. Nary a moment passes that doesn't invite us to both give and receive a special message—a particular lesson. We are always in God's care, and every circumstance of our lives is helping to mold the women we are meant to be.

I will take a long look at where I am today and be grateful for my place. It's right for me, now, and is preparing me for the adventure ahead.

—from *Each Day a New Beginning*

November 7

Accepting God's will as our own simplifies life.

We often hear newcomers or our sponsees ask, "How do I know my will isn't God's will?" Experience has shown us they are the same on occasion. Still, the best response is that we have an intuitively peaceful feeling when we are fulfilling God's will. On the other hand, when chaos invades our inner spaces we are probably acting against God's will in favor of our own.

We hear from seasoned program people that this is a simple program. However, to most of us it feels very complicated initially. We have spent decades learning to be strong, forceful, exemplary managers, invulnerable to hurt and adversity. Now it's suggested that we turn over to God most of what we've spent our lives trying to master. It's not easy to do. We can't fathom how to go about it. But we can recognize conflict when it's occurring, and that may be the best indication to turn to God for guidance.

If I feel good about what I'm doing or saying, or contemplating doing or saying, then I can be fairly certain that God's will is in charge of mine. Today will go as smoothly as my will allows it to go.

—from *A Life of My Own*

November 8

All problems work out—though not always the way you want them to.

—JAMES CASEY

We are relieved of our burdens when we have faith that everything works out. We have the benefit of the past to help us right now if we are filled with worry or fear. While it may seem that we didn't get all we'd hoped for when we were young, we can generally accept that we did get what we really needed. Most of us simply didn't have the wisdom to know what was right for us at the time.

Being impaired physically isn't easy to accept, particularly if we were active our whole lives. The lesson here is not that all conditions in our lives are wonderful. That isn't what "working out" means. Rather, it means that we'll see the "miracle" in our circumstance when we open our mind to God's explanation. The physical realm never supersedes the spiritual in importance. The real message for us and our companions lies in the spiritual realm.

There is purpose in every experience. Problems do work themselves out. We can come to believe this, too.

Whatever I need will come to me today. God can be trusted.

—from Keepers of the Wisdom

November 9

*All sorrows can be borne if you put them into a
story or tell a story about them.*

—ISAK DINESEN

Sharing our experience, strength, and hope with others in
this program helps to clarify for all of us the miracle of
recovery. Telling another woman how we survived the
most awful of experiences lets her know that her life is survivable too. It's not by accident that the founders of AA
stressed the value of telling our stories.

Each time we share an aspect of our own traumatic
past, its sting is diminished. The more we repeat these
awful truths, the less their hold on us. Our storytelling lets
our listeners know that their own experiences are not so
different after all.

What lucky women we are. No longer do we hide ourselves from others. Each conversation with a sponsor,
sponsee, or friend is an opportunity to lighten our load.

*I will tell a part of my story to someone today. She may be helped
by it, and I will be freed from it!*

—from *A Woman's Spirit*

November 10

There are no new truths, but only truths that have not been recognized by those who have perceived them without noticing.

—MARY MCCARTHY

We understand today ideas we couldn't grasp yesterday. We are conscious this year of details of our past that we may have glossed over at the time. Our blinders are slowly giving way, readying us for the truths we couldn't absorb before.

"When the student is ready, the teacher appears." And the teacher comes bearing truths that we need to assimilate into our growing bank of knowledge. The truths we may be given today, or any day, won't always make us happy immediately. We may learn that a job is no longer right for us. Or that a relationship has reached an end. And the impending changes create unrest. But in the grand scheme of our lives, the changes wrought by these truths are good and will contribute in time to our happiness.

Let's celebrate the truths as they come and trust the outcome to God. We are traveling a very special road. The way is rocky. The bends limit our vision, but we will be given all the direction we need.

The truths I receive today will guide my steps. I shall move in peace.

—from *Each Day a New Beginning*

November 11

How we behave is a reflection of how we think.

Anxiously waiting for a certain phone call, dwelling on a cutting criticism, watching for an expected rebuff—these were common behaviors for many of us. Our lives were far too focused on other people. And when they weren't overtly loving us or showing respect, we doubted ourselves, often losing our confidence even in the middle of a task. How others treated us controlled how we thought of ourselves. We seldom considered that others' insecurities caused them to try to diminish us.

Now we are free from their control. We are spending time with people who are seeking a healthier way of life. Using affirmations and strengthening our relationship with our Higher Power are helping us develop healthier attitudes about ourselves. As our self-esteem grows, so will our accomplishments. Not letting others have power over how we'll behave is the ticket to a happier, more successful future. The Twelve Step program is making our independence possible.

I won't be controlled by others' responses. With my Higher Power's help I will be successful today. My self-esteem depends on me.

—from *A Life of My Own*

November 12

*No matter what's going on, what we've sent out
comes back to us enlarged.*

—JEAN WILL

Are we content? Do we have the people and the activities
in our lives that we really want here? Hopefully we can answer yes to these questions. But if we can't, it's not too late
to change our possibilities. What comes to us is a reflection of ourselves. When our experiences don't please us,
let's ponder our role in them because we are reaping what
we have sown.

We can cultivate better experiences. We have it in our
power to change what we send out. That means that what
we get back will be different, too. This isn't new information; we have known this our whole lives. It's called the
Golden Rule. It's possible we never realized how much influence our behavior had on that of others, but we can get
a good example of it instantly. Just offer genuine love and
friendship to someone you have ignored lately and see
what happens.

*I will have as good a day as my attitude allows. That's a powerful
realization.*

—from *Keepers of the Wisdom*

November 13

～○

Let's teach acceptance.

Nothing has the absolute power to control us or destroy us. We may fold under the hostile criticisms of strangers or be daunted by the outrageous actions of friends, but we always have another available response. It's this: We can see every person, no matter who they are, as the Teachers we're ready for. This doesn't mean we won't feel their insults. Nor does it mean we won't resist their lessons. It simply means we can learn to be detached from the particulars of the situation, focusing instead on the opportunity to accept and love even that which injures the ego.

Acceptance isn't as difficult as we may think. Actually, it's a simple decision that bears repeating, as often as necessary. When we choose to accept an experience as a learning opportunity, regardless of its nature, it profoundly changes the tenor of our journey. We're often reminded that the sticky details of our experiences don't matter. Why don't we relinquish our resistance to this idea?

I will accept today's journey as the one I'm ready for.

—from *Daily Meditations for Practicing the* Course

November 14

To stop behaving in a certain way is to risk the unfamiliar.

—JAN LLOYD

Old patterns grip us so tightly! Even when the behavior pinches us painfully, we are loathe to give it up. Its familiarity makes it tolerable, knowable, somewhat manageable, and far less scary than trying something new. However, we are truly the luckiest women alive because now we have a training ground where it is safe to try new behaviors. We can discard old, self-defeating patterns in the safe environment of these Twelve Steps.

We are on this recovery path because each of us wants a new life. We have grown sick and tired of the old ways that no longer work. And we have come to believe that change is possible if we look for it in the right place. This is the right place! At any meeting we can see other women who, like us, are trying on new behaviors and meeting with success. We are role models for one another, and every time one of us tries a new response to an old situation, we are all heartened and stretched a bit. We know that what another can do, we can do too.

I am in the right place today to let go of the old and try the new. My support is all around me. I will not fear.

—from *A Woman's Spirit*

November 15

❧

I believe that a sign of maturity is accepting deferred gratification.

—PEGGY CAHN

It's okay to want to feel good all the time. Happiness is something we all deserve. However, there are often preparatory steps we need to take, a number of which will not bring joy, before we arrive at a place of sustained happiness.

The level of our pain at any particular moment has prompted us to seek short-term highs. And with each attempt at a quick "fix," we will be reminded that, just as with our many former attempts, the high is very short-term.

Long-term happiness is not the by-product of short-term gratification. We don't have to *earn* happiness, exactly, but we do have to discover where it's found. How fortunate we are to have the program guiding our search. We will find happiness when we learn to get quiet and listen to our inner selves. We will find happiness when we focus less on our personal problems and more on the needs of others.

Many of us will need to redefine what happiness is. Understanding our value and necessity to our circle of acquaintances will bring us happiness, a happiness that will sustain us. Gratitude for our friends, our growing health, and our abstinence also sustain us. Sincerely touching the soul of someone else can tap the well of happiness within each of us.

I will find happiness. Searching within myself, I will patiently, trustingly share myself with others.

—from *Each Day a New Beginning*

November 16

❦

A bad attitude makes for a bad life.

We all know people who seem to court disaster. They are frequently in conflict with other people. They get little joy from life. They are critical of most experiences and not happy about most people. Perhaps we are sometimes like these people ourselves.

It's easier to see how others' attitudes affect their lives than it is to recognize how our attitudes affect our lives. But attitude, for all of us, is profoundly influential. We will experience each situation according to the attitude we cultivate. Even though it *feels* as if our attitude simply happens, we orchestrate it. And we can change it. A tiny decision is all that's necessary.

Our lives mirror our attitudes. Our friends who seem more blessed than we are probably nurture that attitude.

I will focus on my attitude today. How I think will be reflected in what I experience.

—from *A Life of My Own*

November 17

I never dreamed my crafts would be known around the world. I simply did them.

—ALICE MERRYMAN

Hindsight probably allows many of us to see how meaningful our seemingly unimportant activities were. Seldom did we imagine the bigger purpose of any single occurrence. But everything fit so neatly, didn't it? This continues to be true. Even when we don't particularly like a situation or when a person gets under our skin, we can decide to believe that there is purpose in the experience. That decision makes our lives so much more peaceful.

There is nothing more important than knowing peace. It may have taken us a while to come to this understanding, but few of us doubt it now. And yet we feel it far less often than we might. Why is that? The answer is simple, and it's the same for all of us: our lack of peace is due to our egos trying to manipulate situations and people who are in our lives. We aren't satisfied with how something is going, and we become intent on changing it. Just as quickly as we make that decision, our peace has escaped us. What might we do instead? Get quiet and wait. Peace will return. The divine is unfolding. Let's let it happen.

My peacefulness is of my own making. What kind of experience do I want today?

—from *Keepers of the Wisdom*

November 18

∾

Sharing our lessons reinforces our growth.

Many people benefit when we share our experiences, and we are at the top of the list. The founders of this program were wise. They knew that the greatest value of sharing one's experience, strength, and hope was that the story-teller was strengthened and inspired by each telling.

Every one of us, no matter how dedicated we are to working the program and using its tools, gets off center occasionally. Perhaps we momentarily forget the importance of humility and rely on ourselves rather than God for direction. It doesn't take long for our lives to feel out of control once that happens.

Helping someone else at the very time we feel unbalanced mysteriously guides us back to our own center. It's almost as though our Higher Power is reaching us through the words we share with someone who is struggling. The result is clarity for both of us.

I will honor the contact a sponsee or friend makes with me today. Every contact is for a purpose.

—from *A Life of My Own*

November 19

*As I recover, I am learning to detach with love and
mind my own business with dignity.*

—KATHY KENDALL

Very few situations actually need our input. On most occasions we can contribute most by observing or listening. Although controlling how others live and think may still appeal to us, we are learning from our friends and sponsors the wisdom of detachment and the necessity for boundaries between ourselves and others.

Our desire to "help" friends make decisions may be rooted in love: we don't want to see our friends get hurt by making wrong choices. But the wisdom of the program tells us that we hurt our friends more by doing for them what they need to do for themselves. While this may be hard to believe at first, we can learn to trust that it is true.

It is enough to live our own lives thoughtfully. We have been given a second chance through getting clean and sober. Now it's time to give our lives all of our attention. Let's free other people to do the same.

*I have enough to do just to live my life today. I can show my love
for others best if I let them live their lives too.*

—from *A Woman's Spirit*

November 20

❧

God knows no distance.
—CHARLESZETTA WADDLES

As close as our breath is the strength we need to carry us through any troubled time. But our memory often fails us. We try, alone, to solve our problems, to determine the proper course of action. And we stumble. In time we will turn, automatically, to that power available. And whatever our need, it will be met.

Relying on God, however we understand God's presence, is foreign to many of us. We were encouraged from early childhood to be self-reliant. Even when we desperately needed another's help, we feared asking for it. When confidence wavered, as it so often did, we hid the fear—sometimes with alcohol, sometimes with pills. Sometimes we simply hid at home. Our fears never fully abated.

Finding out, as we all have found, that we have never needed to fear anything, that God was never distant, takes time to sink in. Slowly and with practice it will become natural to turn within, to be God-reliant rather than self-reliant.

Whatever our needs today, God is the answer.

There is nothing to fear. At last, I have come to know God. All roads will be made smooth.

—from *Each Day a New Beginning*

November 21

You can't let adversity get you down. Keep smiling.
—VIOLET HENSLEY

Violet's smiles certainly fit this category. She lights up rooms with her joy and energy, her fiddle playing and storytelling. We don't all smile quite so easily. Why is that? Some naively assume one's easy, individual circumstances determine the willingness to smile. A few hours with a soul like Violet convinces us otherwise. The work we've done, the environment we inhabit, the struggles we've had or have been free of do not determine our happiness, thus the frequency of our smiles. That's good fortune, in fact.

Smiling is first an attitude and then an action. We don't have to be bubbling over with inner happiness to smile. On the contrary, if something is bothering us, we may discover it will not loom so large if we focus our energy on smiling at a friend or even a stranger. Some would label it miraculous how changed a problem seems when we decide to put our energy into smiling at the passersby in our lives.

The separation we feel from others is what often gives rise to our problems, regardless of their details. Giving a smile and getting one in return diminishes our sense of separation. Problems diminish, too.

How do I feel today? Even a few smiles will lift my spirits.

—from *Keepers of the Wisdom*

November 22

❧

Giving equals receiving.

There's no ambiguity in this statement. In fact, it makes clear what we'll experience moment by moment throughout our lives. The power it gives us is awesome. Why do we so often use this power to our detriment?

If we had only one response to all the situations in our lives, we'd have either peaceful lives or terribly chaotic, painful ones. Because we have two choices, the expression of love or the willfullness to attack, we can get a mixture of both. Even cursory observation would suggest that we vacillate between our two options.

There's no principle that demands we balance the scales between these two. If anything, the *Course* encourages us to choose only love. And if we did, we'd receive an abundance of it in return. What we give, we'll receive. We're in the driver's seat. If our experiences are generally painful, we need to shift gears.

The opportunity to attack others will arise today, but I can choose to love them instead.

—from *Daily Meditations for Practicing the* Course

November 23

My spirituality is becoming more important to me as I get older.

—JOANN REED

Having a spiritual life is more important to some of us than to others. How we grew up might be a contributing factor. If religion was forced on us, we may have rejected it as soon as we left home. Then, *coming to believe* in a force or power outside of ourselves takes willingness. We may not have that, even yet. But if we sense that others among us are feeling more peace than we're accustomed to feeling, we might seek to know why. Perhaps they have sought and found a spiritual path that comforts them.

One thing that's no doubt true for all of us, regardless of how we grew up, is the wish to feel connected to the world around us, to the people in our lives, to the idea that life has held some purpose. On occasion we lose this feeling. For any number of reasons, we become lonely; our separateness from others is all that we can perceive. Even though the spiritual path tells us that we're never alone, that we're always in a state of oneness with others, we may see only our differences. Let's look again if that's the case.

I will find more joy in today if I seek to be with rather than separate from others. I will try to remember that spiritually we are one.

—from *Keepers of the Wisdom*

November 24

We have been called to share this message.

Whoever we are, wherever we are, it's no accident that we are here, now, carrying the message of the *Course*. Something, perhaps the urging of a friend or a passage in a book, maybe our painful perspective or a harmful relationship, led us to the teachings we now revere. And our lives have changed. We can't go back to the old solutions ever again.

This new way of seeing has smoothed the rough edges of our lives. And this transformation has been so gentle. Sometimes we wonder why it took so long to get here. So many of our past problems would never have held so much of our focus had we known what we know now. That realization makes our present awareness all the sweeter.

Sharing what we know now comes so naturally when we keep our minds on love. The more people we touch with the message, the saner and sweeter the journey for us all.

I am part of a bigger picture. Today I can do my part in saving the world by giving only love.

—from *Daily Meditations for Practicing the* Course

November 25

Obsessing keeps us stuck and weakens our spirit.

We must give up trying to figure out other people. What they do is their journey, not ours. When we let their actions take up residence in our minds, we interrupt our own journey.

What we carry in our minds either nurtures us or tires us. We can be either refreshed or smothered by our thoughts. It's easy to forget that we can discard any thought we don't want. Our thoughts are not in charge of us; we are in charge of them!

Learning to quiet our minds will allow us the opportunity to feel the presence of our Higher Power. Getting quiet and going within will help us understand our personal journey and help us be willing to let others have theirs.

My own journey and relationship with my Higher Power are all that need to be on my mind today.

—from *A Life of My Own*

November 26

〰

How can I know God's will for me?

How commonly we fret trying to decipher God's will for us. We make the search quite complicated. We ask first one person and then another what we should do, and then we second-guess the suggestions. We generally evaluate them according to their benefits for us personally and discard ideas that aren't self-serving. The net result is seldom the peace we deserve, the peace that is truly God's will for each of us.

We can make our search easy. All we ever need to do is ask ourselves one question: "Is what I'm about to do or say or think a loving expression?" If the answer isn't yes, we are not fulfilling God's will. And every time we offer love to a friend or stranger, we are. Knowing, as we now do, what God's will for us is every minute promises us the peace we so much deserve. Our changed demeanor will contribute to the peacefulness of everyone else too.

God's will is no mystery. If I want to live it today, my assignment is easy. Give only love.

—from *Daily Meditations for Practicing the* Course

November 27

*The working of someone's mind is what most
fascinates me in life.*

—MARIA REGNIER KRIMMEL

Having an interest in how others think has the potential
of making every encounter intriguing. We can speculate
about people's up-bringings, about their political or spiritual viewpoints. We can appreciate their education and
their openness to differing opinions, or feel dismayed at
their rigidity. There's little that's more important in one's
life than the attention we are willing to give others. We
may not have placed much value on our many personal encounters, but they were not without purpose in our lives.
Being able to appreciate them now offers us a worthy gift.

Most of us have experienced some distinct disappointments in our lives. Jobs weren't as fulfilling as we'd expected. Children disappointed us, perhaps. Marriages were
filled with strife. For many, few dreams ever materialized.
We can lament this collection of memories for the rest of
our lives, or we can opt to make whatever time we have left
more meaningful. The easiest way to do this is to focus
more intently on the individual conversations that engage
us today. They are not simply coincidence. They contain
the messages for the better lives that we desire. Listen up!

*Unless I put myself in the path of other people, I'll not get "the
word" today. Do I really want it?*

—from *Keepers of the Wisdom*

November 28

I am convinced, the longer I live, that life and its
blessings are not so entirely unjustly distributed
[as] when we are suffering greatly we are so inclined to suppose.

Self-pity is a parasite that feeds on itself. Many of us are
inclined toward self-pity, not allowing for the balance of
life's natural tragedies. We will face good and bad times—
and they will pass. With certainty they will pass.

The attitude "Why me?" hints at the little compassion
we generally feel for others' suffering. Our empathy with
others, even our awareness of their suffering, is generally
minimal. We are much too involved in our own. Were we
less self-centered, we'd see that blessings and tragedies
visit us all, in equal amounts. Some people respond to
their blessings with equanimity, and they quietly remove
the sting from their tragedies. We can learn to do both.

Recovery is learning new responses, feeling and behaving in healthier ways. We need not get caught by self-pity.
We can always feel it coming on. And we can let it go.

*Self-pity may beckon today. Fortunately, I have learned I have
other choices.*

—from *Each Day a New Beginning*

November 29

*People who think too much about themselves miss
many wonderful opportunities to help others.*
—ALPHA ENGLISH

Self-absorption is not an unusual trait. In fact, it's likely
that we have to fight against it daily. That's due to the
strength of our egos. They want our undivided attention
and they insist on making all our decisions. Putting others' needs first is never our egos' inclination. We are more
than our egos, however, and discovering this "other, higher
self" has perhaps been the most important lesson in
our lives.

Opening up to our higher selves makes it possible to acknowledge the others in our life. Listening to our higher
selves will change who we can become. We have all experienced this transformation many times throughout our
lives. What we realize is that no matter how many times we
have listened, we don't listen all that naturally, even yet.
The ego's demands diminish little over time. Vigilance regarding which voice we listen to is our assignment. Self-
absorption doesn't reward us. Being available to others
makes us rich beyond our wildest dreams.

My prosperity lies in my offerings of help to others today.

—from *Keepers of the Wisdom*

November 30

*Not all relationships that are right for us
are peaceful.*

Every person we have contact with offers a learning opportunity. It may happen that what we have to learn in some relationships doesn't feel all that pleasant. Even hostile relationships can be purposeful and valuable. Our mission is to heal, and healing occurs through our encounters with others.

It's not unusual to be confronted with the same difficult person day in and day out. The *Course* would say that's not coincidental. The agitation we feel is not about the other person, no matter how strong we desire it to be so. That we come together, again and again, can only mean healing is called for, and healing is possible. Our task is to desire it, seek a new perspective on the struggle, and wait. If we really want help, it will come. If we really want healing, it will happen.

*Today may include some strife with a friend. We can draw closer if
we so desire.*

—from *Daily Meditations for Practicing the* Course

December

December 1

When I feed on resentments and anger, I am giving someone else rent-free space in my head.
—KATHY KENDALL

Becoming consumed by our emotions is all too familiar. It was a favorite pastime before we got clean and sober, and it still may "own" us. Much to our dismay, sponsors remind us that we're getting a payoff or we wouldn't continue the practice. They also tell us it's never too late to give it up.

We can begin immediately. Let's breathe in the positive. It takes the same effort as dwelling on resentments, and the outcome is so much healthier. Let's bring our blessings to mind first. Breathe in the images of friends and the smiles we share. Breathe in the image of our Higher Power and those comforting arms. Breathe in the bright light of healing that is the program's gift. Breathe in the peace that comes with knowing all is finally well.

Giving our minds over to loving images heals us. The hurts of the past can reach us no more if we breathe in the good.

I will breathe in my Higher Power today. I will dwell on the safety and serenity of my journey.

—from *A Woman's Spirit*

December 2

We all are healers.

The miracle of healing, according to this course of study, is simply the decision to shift our perceptions of the people and the experiences surrounding us. None of us has greater healing power than anyone else. Some practice the healing process more often, however.

The one absolute in every day for everybody is that there will be an opportunity to offer a healing gesture to someone or some situation. Just knowing that we can improve the world we live in by a tiny thought or action gives the most mundane of days real meaning. We are equal in our ability to move us all closer to home.

If we look at our experiences from this perspective, it will change how we see every minute of our lives. We'll even begin to look for opportunities to offer healing. Knowing that all of us benefit through the gestures of any one of us inspires our willingness to participate in the miracle.

I have the opportunity to add to the richness of every person's experience today through my perspective.

—from *Daily Meditations for Practicing the* Course

December 3

*Spiritual power can be seen in a person's reverence
for life—hers and all others, including animals and
nature, with a recognition of a universal life force
referred to by many as God.*

—VIRGINIA SATIR

Taking the time, daily, to recognize the spiritual force in
everyone and everything that is all about us encourages us
to feel humble, to feel awe. Reflecting on our interconnec-
tions, our need for one and all to complete the universe,
lessens whatever adversity we might feel as we struggle with
our humanity.

Our spiritual power is enhanced with each blessing we
give. And as our spiritual power is enhanced, life's trials
are fewer. Our struggle to accept situations, conditions,
and other people, or our struggle to control them, lessens
every day that we recognize and revere one another's
personhood, one another's existence.

*I can teach myself reverence, and I can begin today. I will look for
"the Spirit" everywhere, and I will begin to see it.*

—from *Each Day a New Beginning*

December 4

Anger never benefits us.

We've been told that we must express our anger, and that it's necessary to confront whomever is responsible for it. From the *Course* we are learning something quite different. We are learning that anger is the ego on the loose. Anger is never necessary; it is always a cry for healing and help.

What does it mean when we are the brunt of someone else's anger? Shouldn't we at least address it? The *Course* says no. To address it is to make it real, which fosters its manifestation again and again. Our better response is to turn the other cheek, to offer loving forgiveness. Let's not forget that whatever we perceive in the experiences we've attracted directly reflects what we expected, what we projected, and what we actually wanted, even though we may insist otherwise.

No doubt we've all heard someone say, "But anger energizes me." Let's suggest they weigh the long-term results of the empowerment gained when they say no to anger and yes to love. How good it feels to take charge of our expressions.

Anger may try to imprison me today, but I hold the key that opens the door to freedom and peace.

—from *Daily Meditations for Practicing the* Course

December 5

I have a simple philosophy. Fill what's empty.
Empty what's full. And scratch where it itches.
—ALICE ROOSEVELT LONGWORTH

All too often, we complicate our lives. We can wonder and worry our way into confusion; obsession or preoccupation it's often called. "What if?" "Will he?" "Should I?" "What do you think?" We seldom stop trying to figure out what to do, where to do it, how to meet a challenge, until someone reminds us to "keep it simple."

What we each discover, again and again, is that the solution to any problem becomes apparent when we stop searching for it. The guidance we need for handling any difficulty, great or small, can only come into focus when we remove the barriers to it, and the greatest barrier is our frantic effort to personally solve the problem. We clutter our minds; we pray for an answer and yet don't become quiet enough, for long enough, to become aware of the direction to go, or the steps to take. And they are always there.

Inherent in every problem or challenge is its solution. Our greatest lesson in life may be to keep it simple, to know that no problem stands in our way because no solution eludes a quiet, expectant mind.

I have opportunities every day to still my mind. And the messages I need will come quietly. My answers are within me, now.

—from *Each Day a New Beginning*

December 6

It is the long stretch of time that gives us our viewpoint.

—FLORIDA SCOTT-MAXWELL

In the heat of an experience, our emotions own us. Hurt feelings, anger, or fear pushes away the rational explanation of what occurred. It's often not until hours or maybe days later that we understand the dynamics of that moment.

Wishing we could gather all the facts immediately is understandable. It might save us from losing control of our emotions. But learning to step back before responding to an experience takes discipline.

Hindsight is perhaps our best teaching tool. We can review the past and see how every experience, even the most painful, has added to our development. Trusting that the same will be true of whatever appears on our horizon today relieves us of the need to worry and overreact. Since we know we'll understand in due time, let's relax now.

I remember some difficult periods that benefited me. If something troubles me today, perhaps I can trust that it, too, is for my good.

—from *A Woman's Spirit*

December 7

I believe there has been a grand plan for my life; so much has happened that I hadn't counted on.

—LOUISE JEROME

What Louise believes might offer great comfort, particularly to a mind that is fraught with fear and uncertainty. But it's not all that important whether or not we believe that God has planned every detail of our lives. In fact, if we have had more than our share of turmoil, we might feel that God has been punishing us. Just coming to believe that we haven't walked through any experience alone is where the comfort lies. This may not be an idea we were taught as youngsters. We may not be convinced of it now. But deciding to suspend our disbelief, for a time, in order to discover the peace within this idea is worth it.

Recalling our past, any portion of it, will no doubt bring to mind outcomes to situations that took us by surprise. We so often thought we knew what was best for us and others. What folly! What relief, too. Trying to *play god* in others' lives is a heavy burden. We may still be caught in this maze, but getting free of it is possible. It may mean we have to change our perspective on the way life *really works,* the role God plays in our lives, but we can open our minds to new ideas. We're older, for sure, but minds can change at any age. Let's settle for an idea that eases our journey.

Today can be as restful as I make it. What comes to me is right for me.

—from *Keepers of the Wisdom*

December 8

I find myself wondering whether serenity is really attainable for women with small children.

—MARY CASEY

Serenity is a state of mind. Children, animals, co-workers, careers, traffic, ringing phones, bad weather, drinking partners—all can steal our serenity if we let them. Even beautiful weather and loving companions can't guarantee serenity. Deciding to free our minds of the clutter that keeps us agitated is what assures our serenity.

Focusing on our Higher Power and seeking guidance will bring us peace. Even during the most troubling times, we can be at peace if we quiet our minds, focus on the Spirit within us, and remember that our lives are uniquely purposeful. We are needed; we have a specific role to play; in the stillness we can best decipher our particular part.

In the midst of havoc I can find the stillness, if that's my desire.

—from *A Woman's Spirit*

December 9

I heard a story once about an old man who washed his old boat every day. When asked why, he said because he got joy out of it. I like that story. That's why I do what I do, too.

—ALICE MERRYMAN

Experiencing joy from what we do is the best reward of all, isn't it? We might appreciate the monetary results, if there are some, and we are pleasantly touched by compliments from others. But the experience of getting outside of ourselves, getting fully absorbed by whatever the activity is, and feeling joyfully one with it, is the best reason for pursuing any activity. There is some activity that will do that for each of us. Have you found yours yet?

Alice was too busy working on the farm with her husband and raising their children to search for outside interests when she was younger. But as the changes began, changes like those that are inevitable for all of us, she promptly saw that she needed to find meaningful interests. Painting, caning chairs, and making dolls from corn shucks filled her days. She didn't know that she'd be good at any of these things, that she'd gain notoriety, but indeed she did. Her work is in the Smithsonian, she met presidents, she was on the *Today Show*. But what has meant the most to her is knowing real joy. She feels that every day, every time she picks up a paint brush or a corn shuck. What an example she is for us and all who know her.

This day will make me joyful if I do what brings me joy. Do I know what that is?

—from *Keepers of the Wisdom*

December 10

The process of living, for each of us, is pretty similar.
For every gain there is a setback. For every success,
a failure. For every moment of joy, a time of
sadness. For every hope realized, one is dashed.
—SUE ATCHLEY EBAUGH

The balance of events in our lives is much like the balance of nature. The pendulum swings; every extreme condition is offset by its opposite, and we learn to appreciate the gifts of the bad times as well as the periods of rest.

On occasion we'll discover that our course in life has changed direction. We need not be alarmed. Step Three has promised that we are in caring hands. Our every concern, every detail of our lives, will be taken care of, in the right way, at the right time.

We can develop gratitude for all conditions, good or bad. Each has its necessary place in our development as healthy, happy women. We need the sorrows along with the joys if we are to gain new insights. Our failures keep us humble; they remind us of our need for the care and guidance of others. And for every hope dashed, we can remember, one will be realized.

Life is a process. I will accept the variations with gratitude. Each, in its own way, blesses me.

—from *Each Day a New Beginning*

December 11

*We are always in the right place at the right time to
learn what we need to know.*

We worry far too much about how to *do* life! Have I prepared enough for this assignment? Am I the right mate for
this particular person? Did I offer the right example to
those who look up to me? We may have to stretch our willingness to believe that we are exactly where we need to be
all the time. But it's true.

The events of our lives are the classroom for our minds.
That's a refreshing idea. It saves us from regret over the
past. It gives us hope for the present and the future. The
people with whom we come together have something to
offer us. If not love, then the opportunity for us to offer it
anyway. Every experience is a time for healing. We are always the healers as well as the healed. We are never where
we can't be helpful to the others in our midst.

I can overcome fear today if I remember I am where I need to be.

—from *Daily Meditations for Practicing the* Course

December 12

◆

*My accomplishments have been simple and not very
important, but I've had an interesting life.*

—ALICE MERRYMAN

Having an interesting life is what we've all wished for, no
doubt. How we defined "interesting" varied, of course. Advanced education appealed to some. Experimenting in the
garden or the kitchen or the workshop gained the attention of others. Traveling to foreign countries or writing
one's memoirs lent an interesting element to many lives.

Did it matter if our lives seemed interesting to others?
Not really, yet each of us benefited from sharing our interests with others because of what our pursuits had taught
us. Sharing what we had learned with others always gave
them greater meaning. It also helped us remember that we
were a necessary link in the human community.

We are still an important link. Aging makes us doubt
this perhaps, but look around. Friends still call, strangers
still smile at us, children and grandchildren still remember
our birthdays. We have added a richness to others' lives.
Whether most people appreciated all the fruits of our interests isn't so important; that we continued to find meaning in our own lives is what offered a wonderful example.
What better legacy could we leave?

*Today I will reflect on the richness of my experience and
relationships.*

—from *Keepers of the Wisdom*

December 13

Friendships divide our burdens and double our joys.

Having women and men we trust enough to share our deepest secrets with is one of the many gifts of the program. While it's true that most of us already had friends, we seldom told them everything about ourselves. We held back the most intimate details to protect ourselves. We thought if they really knew us, they'd never want to be our friends.

Our understanding of friendship has changed since being introduced to the Twelve Steps. How we act as friends has changed too. Now we know that friends don't judge, they don't try to control, they accept how other people are, and they never betray a confidence. They listen, they love, and they offer hope. And they don't run away when they don't like what they hear. What we have learned influences our old friendships too, and everybody benefits.

To express my friendship fully to someone today means sharing honestly what I'm experiencing and listening intently while my friend shares too.

—from *A Life of My Own*

December 14

My greatest feeling comes from knowing I have had an effect on something.

—JANICE CLARK

The reality is that everything we do or think or say has its effect. Of course it follows that our effect may not always be good. However, Janice is referring to the positive impact she has so often had. Her small Arkansas town owes a debt of gratitude many times over for her hard work. Can the rest of us feel so certain of such an effect?

It's valuable to take an occasional inventory of our many involvements with others. Are we proud of how we behaved in all instances? Did the circumstance get a positive boost from our input? We can be certain it got a boost of some kind! We can also be certain that whatever opportunity we had for acting was not coincidental. There are no coincidences. The invitation for us to act, thus affect situations and people, was quite intentional. Have we always acted in the best interests of others?

All of us have memories of when we didn't do the right thing. Fortunately, we can acknowledge our mistakes and try to repair the damage. Even more advantageous is the realization that we can be free of bad memories in the future if we show great concern about every action we take today.

My life has been quite purposeful. Today's opportunities to act are no different.

—from *Keepers of the Wisdom*

December 15

There were deep secrets, hidden in my heart, never said for fear others would scoff or sneer. At last I can reveal my sufferings, for the strength I once felt in silence has lost all its power.

—DEIDRA SARAULT

There is magic in sharing ourselves with someone else. We learn from Steps Four and Five that what we thought were heinous acts are not unusual. Our shameful acts are not unique, and this discovery is our gift when we risk exposure.

Realizing how much we are like others gives us strength, and the program paves the way for us to capture that strength whenever and wherever we sense our need. Secrets block us from others and thus from God too. The messages we need to hear, the guidance offered by God, can't be received when we close ourselves off from the caring persons in our lives. They are the carriers of God's message.

How freeing to know we share the same fears, the same worries. Offering our story to someone else may be the very encouragement she needs at this time. Each of us profits from the sharing of a story. We need to recognize and celebrate our "sameness." When we share ourselves, we are bonded. Bonding combines our strength.

Silence divides us. It diminishes our strength. Yet all the strength we need awaits us. I will let someone else know me today.

—from *Each Day a New Beginning*

December 16

Knowledge is not the goal of the Course. *Peace is!*

Knowledge has value, but it won't guarantee happiness if we continue to filter our experiences through the eyes of the ego. The ego's purpose is to push us to be more aggressive and controlling in all our relationships. Peace is never that outcome.

If peace is this *Course*'s goal, how can we be certain of attaining it? The steps to take are simple. Every encounter is an opportunity. First, when someone engages us in conversation, if we feel any inkling to judge them negatively, immediately ask the Holy Spirit to help us see them differently. Next, ask the Holy Spirit to give us the words to say or the feelings to project. Then wait for the words and the feelings to come. They will. Always. Our impatience may push us to act too soon, however. We'll have to be vigilant.

I welcome all opportunities for knowing and conveying peace today.

—from *Daily Meditations for Practicing the* Course

December 17

You become more authentically yourself as you get older.

—BETTY FRIEDAN

It probably doesn't take much reflection to remember times we lied to the boss about why a project was late. Or to a spouse or parent about where we were. Or made an excuse to an acquaintance about why we couldn't attend a social function. And the times are numerous when we pretended to agree with an adversary rather than risk losing a promotion or a friendship.

But were we really phonies every time we stretched the truth or kept silent rather than disagree? The answer lies within. The question we must address is how did we feel each time we opted to skirt the truth rather than risk the consequences? If it bothered us, even a little bit, it will be easier to explore our authenticity now.

In the long run, nothing was ever gained by our glazing over the facts. Maybe we "saved ourselves" in the moment, but we chipped away at the soul within. We are free, at last, to be ourselves.

I enjoy real freedom now. The only person I want to impress is me. Being honest is all it takes.

—from *Keepers of the Wisdom*

December 18

Instead of worrying about being different from others, I will love myself for being unique.

—KELLEY VICKSTROM

Where did we learn to compare ourselves with other women? Why is the process so seductive? We seldom measure up, in our eyes. Every woman we see, at first glance, seems smarter or wittier, and certainly more attractive. Self-doubt sets in again and again. Those few times we "win" the comparison test, we feel smug, but the victory is short-lived because another woman soon enters our space.

Meditating often about the gift of uniqueness that our birth guaranteed will bring us closer to understanding that gift. Why would God have made us all unique unless we were here to handle a very special assignment? At first this may not seem realistic. But think for a moment of the women you know in recovery. Are they setting identical goals for their lives? Do they think and act exactly alike? Our lives may be complementary and we may be walking similar paths, but our assignments are unique. God needs each of us for the divine picture to be whole.

I am who I need to be to fulfill my role in this divine world. What I have to offer is important.

—from *A Woman's Spirit*

December 19

You can't imagine how it will come, but everything we need is here for us, and we have to learn to draw it to us.

—JEAN WILL

One of the supreme gifts of growing old is learning to worry less. Only the luckiest among us escaped worrying about our children, our jobs, our spouses when we were younger. We just didn't understand that worry affected nothing except our attitudes and our potential for happiness. How fortunate that time hasn't run out for us. We can develop freedom from worry through a mere decision, made as often as necessary.

From ministers, favorite books, friends' counsel we were told that everything we really needed to fulfill our purpose in this life was available to us. What we had to learn to trust was that the doors to our fulfillment would open when we were ready to pass through them. And they did.

This is still the case. Anything that needs to be handled by us today will beckon. Believing that we are in the right place, right now, makes it so. There is no need for worry. All is well.

I am on God's course for my life. I'll get what I need today.

—from *Keepers of the Wisdom*

December 20

Wisdom never kicks at the iron walls it can't bring down.

—OLIVE SCHREINER

God grants us the serenity to accept the things we cannot change. Many times—yesterday, last week, today, and even tomorrow—we'll come face-to-face with a seemingly intolerable situation. The compulsion to change the situation, to demand that another person change the situation, is great. What a hard lesson it is to learn we can change only ourselves! The hidden gift in this lesson is that as our activities change, often the intolerable situations do, too.

Acceptance, after a time, smoothes all the ripples that discourage us. And it softens us. It nurtures wisdom. It attracts joy and love from others. Ironically, we often try to force changes that we think will "loosen" love and lessen struggle. Acceptance can do what our willpower could never accomplish.

As we grow in wisdom, as we grow in understanding, as we realize the promises of this program, we'll stand ready, as women, to weather all our personal storms. Like the willow in the wind, we'll bend rather than break. And we'll be able to help our sisters become wise through our example.

My lessons are not easy. But they will ease my way. Better days begin today.

—from *Each Day a New Beginning*

December 21

To behave with dignity is nothing less than to allow others freely to be themselves.

—SOL CHANELES

Being either parents or employers makes setting limits on others' behavior second nature. We did it quite appropriately for many years. However, that's not our job anymore. Even when a spouse or a friend chooses to think or act in ways counter to our best judgment, it's not up to us to correct or criticize them. They are responsible for themselves.

Occasionally we experience inner conflict because our values are not shared by loved ones. No matter our age, we relish agreement among our friends, but this just isn't a perfect world. The perspective we have of any situation reflects our own personal history, and none of us share identical histories. Actually, that's quite fortunate. It makes the tapestries of our lives much more colorful.

There are benefits to growing old. We can dare to say what we really think. We can decline invitations or pursue myriad hobbies, answering to no one for a change. The same is true for our friends and family members.

I will be proud of my behavior today, and I'll let others be responsible for themselves.

—from *Keepers of the Wisdom*

December 22

*When the ego is threatened we can expect a battle—
an inner one or an actual one with a companion.*

What is a threatened ego? It's when the ego feels like it's losing control of a situation or some person. The fear of this happening is so overwhelming that the ego attacks whoever is present, sometimes relentlessly. Does it maintain control through this process? Never, at least not for long. The cycle of conflict just keeps repeating itself with nothing gained.

The futility of this process drives some of us to finally ask, "Is there another way?" *A Course in Miracles®* has been offered as our answer. Let's be grateful that Bill Thetford posed the same question. We're the ones able to profit from the reply. *There is another way* and it's so simple. We seek another understanding of the circumstances or the people who seem to be the cause of our discontent. Our perceptions will change. Peace will surround us, providing we want it more than the seduction of control.

If I am attracted to the idea of control at any time today, I'll take note of it and seek a moment of peace instead.

—from *Daily Meditations for Practicing the* Course

December 23

Some people are just determined to be unhappy.
—ALPHA ENGLISH

Have you ever tried to befriend someone who snarled at every circumstance in life? Perhaps a neighbor or an acquaintance from church comes to mind. Generally, we dread getting caught in conversation with them because their negativity occasionally rubs off on us. We can't always avoid people like this, even though we'd prefer to. There is a solution to our dilemma: quietly bless them for reminding us that life is much more pleasant when we seek the brighter side.

Only a pained person sees nothing but the darkness. When we are drawn into his or her circle, let's consider it our assignment to offer a brighter side. We often can't change a person's opinions, but we can avoid strengthening those opinions with our assent. We need not argue with him or her. Simply offer another perspective with a smile. In some instances it won't take much more than this to get a friend to see his or her folly, at least once in a while. Every time we offer another view to a troubled friend, we give him or her food for thought and hope for change.

Nothing can "make" me unhappy today. I can choose my attitude.

—from *Keepers of the Wisdom*

December 24

❧

Carrying the message is our answer too.

The founders of Alcoholics Anonymous, Bill W. and Dr. Bob, knew from firsthand experience the value of telling someone else "what [it] used to be like, what happened, and what [it's] like now." They were graced with sobriety and maintained it as a result of their commitment to carrying their message to other people. Step Twelve asks us to follow their example.

Our message is one of hope. Other people gave it to us when we entered the program, and we maintain hope by telling others how our lives have changed. Perhaps we need frequent reminders of the pain of our struggle to maintain appreciation for how good our lives have become. Being in the program certainly gives us the opportunities. Sharing our stories with others who are troubled helps us too. And if it's their time to accept help, others will gain hope from our stories.

I can keep my hope for a better life by giving hope to someone else today.

—from *A Life of My Own*

December 25

We can trust in the constancy of one thing—time will always move forward, taking us away from the old and gently guiding us to the new.

—AMY E. DEAN

It's human nature to want the pleasurable experiences to last forever and the painful ones to leave immediately. But we can't move through anything faster than the hands of the clock will allow. A better response to our circumstances, regardless of their flavor, is acceptance that God has put a lesson in them for us and we can't adequately judge the long-term value of any of our experiences.

Nothing lasts forever. The slogan "This too shall pass" promises us the emotional relief we need when times are hard. Time is our friend, always, even when we don't like the lesson. We do get what we need, when we need it.

I am on track. What comes to me today is something my Higher Power says I'm ready for. The time is always right.

—from *A Woman's Spirit*

December 26

My lifetime listens to yours.
—MURIEL RUKEYSER

Our experiences educate us to help show each other the way. Others' experiences, likewise, will help still others. We need to share our histories. And the program offers us the way. There is no greater honor we can give one another than rapt attention. We each want to be heard, to be special, to be acknowledged. And recognition may well be the balm that will heal someone's hurt today.

A new day faces us, a day filled with opportunities to really listen to someone who needs to be heard. And the surprise is that we will hear a message just right for us, where we are now. A message that may well point us in a new, better direction. Guidance is always at hand, if only we listen for it. But when we are trapped in our own narrow world of problems and confusion, we scramble whatever messages are trying to reach us. And we miss the many opportunities to make another person feel special and necessary to our lives.

My growth is enhanced every time I give my attention fully to another person. And this process is multiplied over and over and over. I will be there for someone today.

—from *Each Day a New Beginning*

December 27

*Each friend represents a world in us, a world
possibly not born until they arrive.*

—ANAÏS NIN

We are surrounded by women and men who are necessary
for our development. That's a startling revelation perhaps.
We don't even like everybody in our life! How can we need
them? But we do. Our Higher Power clearly understands
our purpose and our needs, and ushers into our lives those
people who will help us grow and change and contribute. It
sounds mysterious initially, but when we get accustomed
to the idea, we are relieved. Each person will teach us something we need to know about life and about ourselves.

Our individual character is growing, changing, maturing. Our understanding of others and our experiences
deepens with each unfolding event. The world is ever-
changing. By design, not coincidence, we will befriend
those people who need us, just as we need them.

*I am where I need to be. My friends and associates need me as I
need them. We are moving and growing in concert.*

—from *A Woman's Spirit*

December 28

Relationships repeat themselves.

Who we encounter is never coincidental. Every person who crosses our paths is a potential learning partner or a temporary control-opponent. In one sense, they serve the same purpose. We share a mission *here,* and we will all complete it, eventually.

Some relationships strike us as hostile, not worth the effort to make them tolerable. More often than not, we learn the most from them. Why is that? No doubt it's because we have to give up our attempts to change them and pray for acceptance. It shouldn't surprise us that when we pray for a different understanding of someone or something, we get it.

We are learning that how we see one person influences how we see everyone else. Perhaps we hadn't noticed that before, but if we were prone to judging someone, we quite easily fell into judging, at least on a small scale, even those we claimed to love fully. It might be said that we really have only one relationship in this entire experience of life. Healing it will heal them all.

I will take the opportunity to heal every relationship by deciding to teach only love today.

—from *Daily Meditations for Practicing the* Course

December 29

Stop and think...

A good habit to develop is deciding to stop and think before reacting to an accusation or contrary opinion, or before taking action in any situation. Taking a few seconds to deliberately pause and quiet ourselves before speaking will keep us from complicating our relations with others.

The need to be right is human nature. But just because everyone struggles with this issue doesn't mean we should excuse it in ourselves. Pausing to ask ourselves, "Is this really worth arguing over?" will help most of us make the decision to back off, to let go, to choose peacefulness instead. Once we begin doing this regularly, we'll sense the power it gives us, power to decide who we will be every moment. Our confidence and self-worth will reflect this healthy empowerment. We'll never want to go back to our old ways.

I will begin the day with a quiet mind. I will go within before responding to others today.

—from *A Life of My Own*

December 30

~❧~

*Women sometimes gossip when they want to get
close to people.*

—JOAN GILBERTSON

Feeling alone and lonely heightens our fears of inadequacy.
In our alienation from others, paranoia grips us. We yearn
to feel a connection with someone, and gossip about another someone can draw two lonely people close. We are
bonded.

We need a sense of belonging, every one of us: belonging to the neighborhood; belonging to the staff where we
work; belonging to the group we call friends. Knowing
that we do belong fosters the inner warmth that accompanies security, well-being. And our fears are melted.

The program's Fifth, Ninth, and Tenth Steps guarantee
that we'll feel the closeness we long for when we work
them. Self-revelation strengthens our ties to the people
we long to connect with. Gossip loses its appeal when we
know we share a closeness already. Mingling our vulnera-
bilities secures our closeness.

We need to be attentive to our judgments of others, be
they verbalized in gossip or only savored in silence. These
judgments act as barometers of our own self-image. Our
security in knowing we belong, that we are one, relieves us
of the need to judge others unfairly.

*Loneliness pushes me to behavior that even compounds the loneli-
ness. Real closeness will come when I talk about myself rather
than someone else.*

—from *Each Day a New Beginning*

December 31

Death, I now see, may not come when I am eighty-five and weary. . . . It will come whenever it damn well pleases.

—JOYCE WADLER

Seldom do we pause to absorb the fact of our mortality thoroughly. The unexpected death of an acquaintance can shock us into this realization, but it's far better to remember that all we have is now.

Using this recovery program to guide our thinking and our behavior helps us live more in this moment. The slogan "One day at a time" specifically addresses our need to be here, now. Deciding that our destiny is in the reliable hands of our Higher Power gives us a respite from worrying about the future. The miracle of our specific recovery, particularly in light of all those who don't receive the gift, should convince us that our journey is by design. So is our death.

I have today. I'll make the most of it and leave the future to God.

—from *A Woman's Spirit*

About the Author

KAREN CASEY is the best-selling author of *Each Day a New Beginning, Daily Meditations for Practicing the* Course, *Keepers of the Wisdom,* and numerous other books. She has also written two books for girls: *Girls Only!* and *Girl to Girl.* Her signature book, *Each Day a New Beginning,* has sold three million copies. Casey enjoys golfing and riding her Harley with her husband. She lives in Minneapolis, Minnesota, and Naples, Florida.